From Mafia Boss to the Cross

An Autobiography

by

Dr. Bruno Caporrimo

AuthorHouse™
1663 Liberty Drive, Suite 200
Bloomington, IN 47403
www.authorhouse.com
Phone: 1-800-839-8640

© 2007 Dr. Bruno Caporrimo. All rights reserved.

No part of this book may be reproduced, stored in a retrieval system, or transmitted by any means without the written permission of the author.

First published by AuthorHouse 7/23/2007

ISBN: 978-1-4343-2355-2 (sc)

Printed in the United States of America
Bloomington, Indiana

This book is printed on acid-free paper.

TABLE OF CONTENTS

INTRODUCTION..vii

PART 1

1. The Beginning of My Journey 1
2. Tragedy on Christmas Day..5
3. Police Violence Behind the Scenes.............................10
4. Gambling and Stealing to Pay the Debt....................14
5. A Little Fish in Big New York City 21
6. Exposing the Deception and Control of the Mafia 32
7. You do the Crime, You do the Time 47
8. Beaten and Tortured in Las Vegas 52
9. New Life in California Destroyed by Drugs..............56
10. The Invasion of the Sweet Love of God 65
11. Heaven Opened and the Fire Came Down...............76
12. Visitation of Angels 87
13. Witness and Pass Out Tracts in Casinos....................94
14. Tragedy and Disappointment Coming My Way, But Never Defeated 103

PART 2

15. Italy Mission Miracle..117
16. The Future Ministry - Asia 123
17. Taking on the World for the Master 130
18. Heavenly Crown on His Head 136
19. Upcoming Mayor of Taipei 143
20. Fourth Mission to China..150
21. December 21, 2000: Mission to Break Chains 156

v

22. 2001: Mission to Italy with Morris Cerullo Ministry 165
23. 2001, September End Time Mission to Asia 180
24. December 2004: Invitation to N.Y.C. 191
25. 2005, August 17: Another Blowout! 202
NOTE FROM THE AUTHOR 205
BRIEF BIOGRAPHY 209

INTRODUCTION

Although some of the stories contained in this work are based on real life events, many of them have occurred more than forty years ago. This was my dark side, prior to coming to Christ. I do not condone many of the stories. My purpose, rather, is to reveal my past AND the transformation of my journey from darkness into his marvelous light. Many characters in this work are fictitional and names have been changed to protect the innocent. Persons, living or dead, who portray a resemblance or likeness to some of the characters in this book are coincidental in nature. Now, may God truly bless you as you read of MY life's journey- from Mafia Boss to the Cross.

Dr. Bruno Caporrimo

PART 1

1
THE BEGINNING OF MY JOURNEY

In the beginning I, Bruno Caporrimo, was born in 1941 in Palermo, Sicily. I was one of seven in my family. I was born in the time when Hitler occupied Italy. The dictator Mussolini allied with Hitler while the war was going on. My father was an importer, exporter and an ambassador. He was very well respected in the community and with the government leaders and he was very successful in the agricultural business. He was an importer and exporter of fruits and vegetables. We lived on six acres in a castle with more than sixteen rooms, a mansion. We had no lack. In 1943, when the American soldiers came prior to the liberation of Italy, Mussolini was the General of Italy. He was a personal friend of my family. As the story goes, I was told that in 1941 on my birthday, there were over 100 families celebrating my water baptism. My father had over 300 people working for him on this occasion. We were very wealthy and even Mussolini came to this great banquet. During this time Mussolini was a general in Italy and a brilliant leader. He gave me many gifts for my water baptism. Tragedy begins as the Germans invaded Italy. With no way to go or nowhere to run, such a powerful antichrist dictator Hitler took the nation of Italy. The King and Mussolini the General, allied together under the deception of this false empire. Mussolini came to Sicily and invaded the hills. He entered the villas to our property. He came with German soldiers to recruit my father and his men.

Dr. Bruno Caporrimo

I barely remember as a little boy. I was three years old. Mussolini gave my father greetings and they had a meeting on top of the mountain. He declared to my father, "Antonio, we've been friends for many, many years. Surrender to the Germans and you will not be destroyed." My father had over 300 soldiers with him. We were given three hours to make a decision to surrender peacefully or escape. My family was faithful and patriotic to Italy. My father did not surrender to the will of the Germans. As proud Italians we had no choice but to run to the hills. The next 3 years, as I remember, we spent in caves while the war was going on. The German troops cut ALL the supply lines from the American soldiers who were already occupying Sicily.

The Marines got word to my father that they were in need of supplies and my father became a champion and a leader. He rushed to the rescue and he began to smuggle trucks full of food and all kinds of fruit, rice, and vegetables into the American camps. All of my family were considered heroes to the Americans. As a matter of fact one of these Marines, Ed Welch, fell in love with my mothers' sister and two years later he married her. He was a strong American hero and through him we obtained many favors. After the war we redeemed the land but there was no food left and no money. Everything was destroyed and there was a famine in the land. I remember that when I was five years old, I weighed 18 pounds. I was real skinny since I had not had any food for 12 days. My father finally contacted someone that had bread so he sold 90% of our property. He sold everything except for the castle which we lived in. He signed over the title to the land for three pounds of bread. Today the land is valued at billions of dollars. In 1945 we began to cultivate the land yet it was very difficult. We never recovered the wealth and prestige we had before. Instead, we lost it all and at seven years old I was adopted by my Godfather, Giovanni La Rosa. This man was our neighbor and he kept his land and a small castle on six acres of land where they raised me up. They took me in as their own son. Dear reader, through wars nobody wins except for satan, and lives are destroyed and changed forever.

After years of struggles, my family came to a conclusion to evacuate to America. My mother, my sister, and my brother evacuated to America. I was left behind with my father for more than seven years. At the age of 5 I had a dream to become a minister but the war changed everything. At 13 years old I began to dream of becoming an attorney in Italy. My dream was shattered because my father decided to abandon everything and move to America. On the 13th of December 1958, I joined my family in America, against my will. I left my family, school, work, church and country. Everything that I had loved was taken away from me. When we arrived in New York City my father told me to kneel down and kiss the ground of America. My dad was very traditional. No one in my family was born again except my mother. When I arrived in America, as a young boy, I became very depressed. I had no friends. I just had my family. I remember that it was very cold and I was not very happy about leaving my country. I felt that my dreams were shattered because I left all my friends behind, in my home land.

Hosea 4:6
My people are destroyed for lack of knowledge: because thou hast rejected knowledge, I will also reject thee, that thou shalt be no priest to me: seeing thou hast forgotten the law of thy God, I will also forget thy children.

John 10:10
The thief cometh not, but for to steal and to kill, and to destroy: I (Jesus) am come that they might have life, and that they might have it more abundantly.

I remember my father saying, "Thank God". He made me kneel down and kiss the ground, at the airport, when we arrived in America. I did, and then my father said to me, "Now in America we don't talk in Italian anymore. We have to speak English." I said "Okay, papa." Dear Reader, I am reminded that I did not understand English at all. I was very happy to be reunited with my family. They bought a house in New Jersey. It was very beautiful and I remember that it was Christmas Day. We had a great celebration. Everybody was happy except for me. All I was thinking of was my friends in Italy, my school, and the fun I had as a young boy. Now I was in a strange land. I didn't speak the language and it was very cold. The girls looked like boys. They wore shorts and chewed bumble gum. They had freckles and pimples on their face and the boys looked like girls, with long hair. I found myself locking myself

Dr. Bruno Caporrimo

in my room reading Italian stories and magazines. I always loved to read and I always liked to write. I wanted to become a famous lawyer someday. That was one of my dreams. I went through three months of depression where I locked myself in my closet.

Finally the time came. My brother knocked on the door and he looked at me eyeball to eyeball and said, "Bruno get a job, mommy has cancer and we need money." When he told me that something happened inside me. I remember, at 4 a.m. I was up on a cold December day, there was snow on the street and I did not have the right shoes. In Sicily there is no snow. I went out looking for a job. By 9 a.m. I found a job with a fashion company named Evans-Picone. It was a very famous company. My position was running boy. I was assigned to bring the clothing material from one person to another. Very friendly people worked there, and many of them day after day would teach me English. I worked six days a week, 10 hours a day, for 90 cents an hour. I brought all the money home to support the family. Within seven months, my mother was operated on her stomach. The cancer grew worse. Because nobody knew how to pray and nobody knew to call upon Jesus and nobody had faith, within two months, my mother passed away. I felt like the lights in my life were shut off. I became more depressed and frustrated. I was upset with the doctors and their system, and I was bitter towards God because I lost my mother.

In 1960, I quit my job. Me and six neighbor friends decided to go to California. We rented an apartment and we picked oranges and strawberries in the farm to survive. It was the days of the Beach Boys. All the guys began to party and to drink and chase girls. I was the only one working and paying the bills. After three years of this crazy life, I got a phone call that my father was dying. I sold my 1959 Ford Retractable, which now, is valued at $75,000. We sold it to a Ford dealer for $1100 and we got a 1948 Plymouth. Seven of us began our journey back to New Jersey. It took five cars before we got there because every car was a lemon and leaked oil. This was incredible. We lived like gypsies. It took us 11 days to get back to New Jersey. I arrived in New Jersey and I started working at a construction company. At night I was attending classes to achieve my high school diploma. I moved in with my sister and brother-in-law.

2
TRAGEDY ON CHRISTMAS DAY

Tragedy struck my family again. I was so taken back by that because the love that I had for my mother was very great and I would have done anything for her. I want to remind you that there was no prayer life in my family. No one knew how to pray for healing miracles. Shortly after, my father died broken hearted because of my mothers death. We went to the hospital on Christmas day and the doctor could not find anything wrong with my dad. He was brokenhearted and fell into a deep depression. He gave up his will to live and a priest administered the last rites. Within hours my dad was pronounced dead. It was Christmas Day and for many years Christmas did not have any value for me. There was all this darkness in my journey of life until much later in 1985, when I came to Christ, which will be told in the coming chapters.

I found myself without family values or a mentor. I was lost. All I knew how to do was to work with my hands. I was young, strong, and I worked seven to eight hours a day with a pick and shovel with my brother-in-law in construction. At night, I had no goals and no values. I began to follow a destructive lifestyle. Alongside me came a fellow who was the same as myself. A friend with no direction. His name was Ricky O'Ricchio. He was a wonderful Italian man, very handsome and smart in his own way. He would always chase girls. He came from a family that loved to drink beer, day in and day out. We lived in New Jersey where the law was that you had to be 21 years old to drink alcohol. In

New York State the law was only 18 years old. So my friends and I would get into a car and drive over to New York, to the clubs, to drink and dance. At that time it was the common thing to do. Many of us carried false identification and so it was easy for us to live a lie and get our way. In many clubs 10 cents would buy a large glass of beer. We would have a good time drinking and dancing until after midnight when we were all drunk. When it was time to leave we still had to drive 45 miles to our home in another state.

We would do this week after week. One night, after the club closed, we got into a fight with the bouncer who was a bald man and big and strong. They beat us to a pulp. We fought back but to no avail. We never remembered how we got home. Did we learn our lesson? No, we would go back to other clubs and do the same thing over and over. The worst tragedy of this story is that my friend, Ricky O'Ricchio, loved to drink and drive fast. One night we were coming home from the club on a two way highway. He felt challenged to pass a slow car just as another car was coming from the other direction. At 70 miles per hour Ricky then swerved and flipped over many times. He was thrown out of the car and hit a rock. He suffered a brain coma and died one month later. Family and friends were brokenhearted over this tragedy. Ask yourself this question: "Did they quit drinking?" No, we only stopped for a month, then we went back to drinking even harder. I didn't stop drinking until I became a Christian many years later, in 1985. As a matter of fact, if you want to know more about the subject you can go to my web site and get one of our books called, "The Snake in the Glass", about the deception of alcohol and facts on fermentation.

The Bible declares in Proverbs 23:30-35:
Those who linger long at the wine, those who go in search of mixed wine, do not look on the wine when it is red, when it sparkles in the cup, when it swirls around smoothly; at the last it bites like a serpent, and stings like a viper. Your eyes will see strange things and your heart will utter perverse things. Yes, you will be like one who lies down in the midst of the sea, or like one who lies at the top of the mast, saying "They have struck me, but I was not hurt. They have beaten me, but I did not feel it. When shall I awake, that I may seek another drink?

From Mafia Boss to the Cross

If I would have known then what I know now, I would not have wasted those precious years of my life. How much better to be a part of Christ for a good cause, and not a part of Satan, the serpent of destruction? Unfortunately I was still in darkness. God did not hit it over my head yet and I was still walking in darkness. There was no truth in my life. My soul was totally deceived and I began to lose my conviction of self-worth and my sense of values because I was looking at people that had no faith in God, laws, and to do right instead of wrong. I was around 21 years old, working and going to school to get my high school diploma. As time passed, doors began to open for me and I would take the opportunities I had. I would go dancing and clubbing. From New Jersey, we would cross into New York City to go drinking in the clubs week after week. I was without God's council in my life and come to think of it, now that I look back, Satan was planning my life down a road of destruction. In New York City, on 45th street in Manhattan, there were these VERY famous nightclubs called, "Wagon Wheel" and "The Peppermint Lounge". These clubs were KNOWN for being frequented regularly by super famous movie stars and celebrities like Dean Martin, Frank Sinatra, Sammy Davis Jr., Chubby Checker and also by investors, from all walks of life. These clubs were also known in New York City as being affiliated with mafia, mobsters, the underworld of Manhattan nightlife. I began to associate with this real colorful world that existed. I worked five days a week like a slave and I desired to have pleasure and fun and I was looking to find me a girl, to complete my life. I want to repeat that without a mentor and family values, I was looking in the wrong place. I had a great time among high society people from all over the world, at least this was what I thought. Week after week, I began to drink and live the lifestyle of a social drinker complete with drunks and constant fighting.

One night I was at a club, in a fight, with the bad guy. Sal, one of the owners said to me "You're good with your hands, do you have a suit?" "Yes I do", I answered. "Good", he replied and hired me as one of his bouncers. I was overwhelmed and in my glory, man was I flying high in this entrapment, that seemed to be the right thing to do. The truth is that I was caught in a snare of the devil leading me deep into corruption with the mafia. Night after night I saw people drink and become incredibly drunk. Some I would have to remove from the club due to their terrible behavior. The more these troublemakers were prohibited from entering, the more aggressive and outraged they became. There were many educated people of class whom I was observing. Wealthy people, happy people, the very educated, they would all come into the club sober and go into a 3 day drinking bash and leave beaten, robbed, abused and brokenhearted. Some were even killed after a brawl or fight. These events, you don't see them in a local town, like maybe where you are from dear reader. New York law at that time said that, if the police saw a person out of control, that person could be arrested and booked into jail for 3 days before release. This is all the law ever did for drinking. But we know that this is not the remedy. Isn't it amazing the stronghold demon alcohol has on so many?

Day after day, week after week, month after month, and year after year, people are entrapped by this spirit of darkness. I know...because I, Bruno Caporrimo, lived this lifestyle for many years. Despite the drinking I had to keep myself in good physical shape to keep my position at the club.

One night I came to the club and a big fight was in progress involving a motorcycle gang. I rushed to help out when I noticed many customers taking shelter under the tables. One was Sylvester Stallone, and another was Ed Sullivan. At that time, Mr. Stallone was not famous (today he is one of Hollywood's great actors). I thank God we were able to break the fight and rescue these men.

As a Minister of the gospel of Jesus Christ, I hope and pray that the contents of this book will help people to understand and know how to make good and wise decisions in order to change their lives for the good. It wasn't until 1972 that I left this crazy lifestyle and moved west, seeking the truth, and opened a deli/restaurant in Southern California. For 13 years I sought the truth, yet I was still drinking and blind to the truth. People from ALL OVER the world would come to these famous night clubs. People would line up outside the door. There, I met people in the fast lane. In the uptown night life of Manhattan, New York City.

I began to know gamblers, prostitutes, pimps, the police, violence, the bribes that were going on and from time to time I began to wonder, "What's going on in this world? Who am I? Where am I going?" It was right there that I began to doubt the system, the laws, the country and everything it stood for because of the immorality and destruction and the evils that were going on, night after night. In my spirit I felt that there had to be a better way and that I would not give in to drugs or gambling. I was keeping my integrity away from the evils of drugs, stealing or doing wrong. Every week, after the night club would close, many members of the club would get together. Both blacks and whites would engage in gambling dice or playing cards, all night long. They would always invite me into their activities. I would always reject the offers. I kept my integrity.

3
POLICE VIOLENCE BEHIND THE SCENES

In the winter of 1963 I had no work. There was no construction work and I wanted to find myself a job. I read an article that the World's fair was coming to New York City. Seven days later I applied for any kind of work. They gave me a job driving a trolley cart. It was very exciting. The night before I started working, we were celebrating in the club with some of the people that I was acquainted with. This guy Johnny that I was spending time talking with, I knew from his reputation that he was a gambler and con-man. He was involved in pimping women and many other strange activities. That night, in the restaurant, I said that I had a terrible headache. He handed me a pill and said, "Take this pill. It will get rid of your headache." This was a big mistake that I made. You're probably saying, "But Bruno you have made a lot of mistakes already." I know that, that is why I am writing this book. I took it and swallowed it. I found out later that night that it was LSD. I began to hallucinate and I found myself riding in the car with him. He got involved in a dispute with some men. I remember him exchanging words and then there was a fist fight. All I did was try to break it up and I got punched as well. Then I remember that I ran. I got on the subway and went home.

Three days later, low and behold, this man was with the police pointing me out at the club and saying that I was one of the guys who assaulted him. There the police took me in and questioned me. This was the first time that I was ever involved in the crime life and now I'm being confronted by the police. The police knew my name and wanted to know about this guy "Johnny" who started the fight. I replied to the police, "I don't know this guy Johnny." They started screaming at me the other guys name. I told them that I didn't know where he lives or his last name. That I only knew him from the club. Suddenly, beyond my wildest dreams, the police began to punch me and kick me and say "You're just like Al Capone. You don't know when to pay your tax." I fell to the ground and six of them began to kick me in all of my ribs and all of my body and they continued to question me and pressure me about the other guys name, "Now tell us who this guy is or we'll kill you."

Dear reader, this was beyond my dreams. I never believed the police would be so violent. I had only seen in films of people being beat up and questioned. During the years that I had lived in America, I noticed that the local police were kind and friendly, but now I saw another side. This time it was me and it was for real. This went on for two hours. I had my nose busted, and my face scarred, I was bleeding from my mouth and they threw me in the cell without a phone call to my family, without notifying anybody. They threw me in the cell and booked me for assault, 3rd degree. I was in so much pain that I slept for 2 days in semi-coma. I felt betrayed and abandoned and the world was sinking in. They contacted my brother and they set up a $3,500 bail to get me out. I never got the job at the World's Fair. Now, I am out on bail and I am faced with a criminal charge and I really had no concept or knowledge of criminal cases. We hired an attorney and he asked for $3,000 and he told me that this was a simple assault and that it was no problem, he would get me out. We believed him. After going to the court the third time, without any witnesses or trial, he advised me to plead guilty to a misdemeanor and he said that if I plead guilty they would dismiss the case and send me home since this was my first offense ever.

The enemy lied to me again. Satan was at work. This attorney did not tell the truth or obey the laws. I found this out later. I decided to plead guilty and I went before the judge and the judge asked me what had happened and I remember saying to the judge, "Your honor three were fighting. He punched me and I punched them and we all ran and went home." The judge responded immediately "ok" and the judge gave me six months in jail. Before I could say anything to my attorney, the jailer grabbed me and handcuffed me and took me into the cell room. There once again, frustration, confusion, and fear kicked in as well as hatred. Dear friend, do you see that I was sold under the table. I felt that there was no justice, no God, no jurisdiction system, and that afternoon they handcuffed my feet with chains to my stomach and they put me in a wagon and onto a boat. We crossed an island called, "Riker's Island" 20 miles out of New York City. While I was in the boat, in this very large cage, there was a black man talking to another black man. He shouted out loud, "When I come out of here, I'm going to kill my lawyer." The response from the other inmate was, "Why brother?" The man responded, "Because he stood behind me and sold me out, he told the judge to give me three years." The man shouted, "What was his name?" He said, "His name is Ricky Cohen." As I heard this it dawned on me that this was my lawyer. Rage took over my heart and I began to plan out how I would get even with him. There, I spent 4 months out of six. I tried to occupy my time taking high school classes to learn English. I felt that I had a lot of time on my hands. In this block they put me in, there were 500 inmates. Day after day, the people gambled and played cards and I began my addiction. Inside, I met the Gambino Family. One of the Gambino Family, called Louie, was in his sixties and he was a very short man. They would smuggle for him cheese, food, steaks, and many other things that he needed. He knew about my case and he was very kind towards me.

There was the Black Section, in which 90% of the inmates were Negro, 6% Hispanic, and 4% white. The white, which was the mafia, ruled. The majority of the Negro's, they could not afford a lawyer and would all end up with a stiff sentence. This was before Martin Luther King and the rights. And many of them were not even guilty. Me, being born in Italy, I didn't have this problem. We don't see this on radio or television. Now, in jail, I'm learning that the Negro doesn't get justice. I grew more bitter against the police system and the United States. I hope that you can understand this. There are many people that reach down times in their life. We see that in the Bible, with the story of Joseph. With Daniel, Meshach, Sesach, and Abendigo. Now I'm facing, 'Abadnegro' and BadBruno'! Being that I was new, young and good looking, one of the mafia leaders was after me wanting to rape me. Day after day he would provoke and pick on me. He finally cornered me. I ended up fighting this man and, while fighting him, I busted his nose and face. The police rushed in and they put me in the hole. I spent 30 days in the hole eating bread and water. While I was inside there, I vowed that I would never trust the police and the system, and never be poor again. I have recently read many stories of people finding the Lord Jesus Christ but this was not the case with me. The days were long and lonely, no lights, no food. I couldn't even brush my teeth or wash my face. For thirty days I was treated worse than a pig. My penalty was too much for me. I did not know how to forgive or forget. I vowed that when I came out that I would kill the attorney that sold me and betrayed me. Every night I recited the case of how this attorney sold me to the judge and then the time came for my liberation. I remember getting off the island, taking a bus, and entering the office of the attorney, intending to strangle him. He was sitting in his desk. When he saw me, he had this fearful look in his face and I said, "You sold me out". He had so much fear that he went under the desk. I remember spitting in his face and said, "You're not worth it for me to kill you and go back to jail". There I felt released and walked out of that office a freed man. Even though I didn't know the Lord, I believed that God was with me always.

4
GAMBLING AND STEALING TO PAY THE DEBT

With no plans for my life I felt real alone in this world. I wrote a letter to my brothers and sisters. I told them to forget about me. To not bother looking for me and not to worry about me because I was the first criminal in my family. I had a criminal record and I felt ashamed. I went to downtown New York City where, before, I had met a man who ran a gambling house. His name was Joe Love. He was with the Gambino family and he ran an underground nightclub in New York City. They gave me a place to stay and the gambling addiction became stronger in me day after day and night after night. I see now, looking back, that satan was promoting me. Only I was not aware of it because in my Catholic religion I was taught that satan was not real. The Bible says that satan is real and that he is the enemy of God and of humanity and that he comes to kill, steal and destroy (John 10:10).

Now as I became a gambler and lived in this night life like a rat, from time to time, I would go to different clubs in New York City which were all run by the mafia. Many of them had to pay off the police to operate. As time passed, I was invited to go to a club. The man who was running the place was named Louie Greco. He was a small time gangster. There I gambled for three nights, blackjack, and they lent me $10,000 which I lost. They gave me three days to pay the debt. On the third day this man, Peppy, came looking for me. He came to collect the debt. He replied, "You pay the debt or you die". That day, I got into a physical fight with him and took the gun away from him and ran. As a young man, I had nowhere to go. The police, on one side, beat me up and I could not trust them any longer. On the other side, the mafia wanted to kill me. I did not know what to do. While I was hiding underground I met Ricky DiAngelo. He was a professional jewel thief. He knew my problem. He invited me to go with him. There, we went to one of the best hotels in New York City and we pulled a robbery. We robbed very famous people of their jewels. He took me to the jewelry and garment district. Here was where the wealthiest and most expensive and famous jewelry stores were. This was on 46th Street in Manhattan. We sold the jewelry. We got $25,000. In my heart, I said I was never going to steal again. I had fear and I knew it was wrong. I had conviction in my heart and soul. We went back to Louie Greco and I paid my $10,000 debt. They treated me like a big man. Because of my pride I did not learn my lesson. I began to gamble with them for over two days drinking coffee, and smoking. I lost my $5000 plus they lent me another $15,000. With this big debt looming over me, me and Ricky DiAngelo went back out. I found out that Ricky had all the contacts. He had all the master keys to the most luxurious hotels in New York City, Las Vegas, Florida, Chicago and we went out and pulled other robberies and we were becoming professional jewel thieves.

One of my hobbies and escapes from my darkness and nightmares was shooting pool. Frequently I spent time in pool halls. One of these locations in New York City was on 7th Avenue in Times Square. It was called 'Lucky 7'. This place was where Jackie Gleeson and Paul Newman shot the movie "The Hustler". One afternoon as I was there the attendant got my attention and said, "Bruno, there's a phone call for you." I answered the phone and a lady on the other end said, "I'm looking for your partner Ricky". I replied, "I haven't seen him for a couple of months". She said, "Are you as bad as he is?" I said to her, "Worse" and I laughed. I said, "What's your name?" She said, "Betty". I asked her, "Are you Ricky's girlfriend?" She said, "No". I said, "There is a movie out tonight called '2001'. I have two tickets, would you like to go?" She hesitated and said, "Okay, pick me up at 7 p.m."

Well, at 7 p.m., I drove to her apartment in downtown Manhattan. There, I saw Betty for the first time. She was beautiful, she was blond and blue eyed. She looked like someone you only see in movies. I was stunned at her appearance. I was taken by her makeup and perfume. We had dinner and we watched a movie together and we started to knit together. That night when I walked her up to her door, I asked her if she wanted to go to the park the following day. She replied, "Yes." We had a good time in the park. We both ate a late lunch together. On the second date we kissed. Romance was in the air. She told me she was a virgin and I respected that. On our fifth date, she broke down and cried and told me that she was pregnant by Ricky. When I found out she was pregnant, I contacted Ricky and he informed me that he did not want anything to do with her and that she was just another target. I felt in my spirit that I wanted to help Betty.

At that time, abortion was legal in Florida. I encouraged her to keep the baby. She insisted that she would have an abortion. I didn't want that so I drove her to Florida. We drove for two days and I told her that I was a jewel thief and that I was willing to drive her to Florida. I told her that she could have an abortion and that I would target some high rank hotels to steal some jewelry from the wealthy. My desire was to make love to her. I wanted to have a sexual romance with her. I felt that I was in love and that I would love her with or without the baby. I was driving a 1955 Cadillac. As we arrived in downtown Miami, I rented a little bungalow apartment. Betty made the appointment with the doctor and I went to a famous hotel. I was successful and stole over $200,000 in jewelry.

On the second day, Betty and I enjoyed the sun and the bungalow. We decided to stay a few more days so she could recover from the surgery. On the fifth day I was looking for my younger brother, Sal. He was a private investigator in Miami. I was looking for him because I didn't have his phone number. I went downtown to one of the coffee shops. When I asked for Sal, two undercover police stopped me and asked for my license. They arrested me and they confiscated the car. I had had over $200,000 in stolen jewelry in the car. They took me to the downtown police station and they began to question me. They wanted to know where my brother was. I was shocked. I said "my brother is an investigator. He works for you guys". Apparently though he and his investigative organization were involved with a 'French Connection', a big drug market from Cuba. The police were looking for my brother for questioning and they were really upset.

Again the conversation got a little bit hot. I suspected that the relationship with my brother was friendly but apparently they were not getting along. I was not aware of the facts and then suddenly, just like before in New York City, the police began to torture and punch and kick me. They smashed my head against a wall while demanding that I give them my brother's address or any other people that I was with. They even asked me for local addresses. They wanted to know where I lived. I did not tell them because I wanted to protect Betty. I had a New York drivers license though and after they beat me real good and busted my face up and pulled hair from my head, they said, "You're not coming out of here unless you tell us where your brother is." Then they pushed me into a cell. I was there for three or four days and I managed, through another inmate, to send a note to Betty. A few days later, Betty called me in prison. To my surprise she told me that my brother managed to contact her and that he would drive her back to New York City. Meanwhile, I was in the prison for twenty days.

They never booked me. They never read me my legal rights. Even though the law says they must book or release you in 72 hours. I was totally abandoned. Twenty days passed when, finally, I called my brother Joe in New Jersey. He told me, "What's going on? Where are you?" I told him that I was in jail and that they were holding me until they found Sal. My brother said, "You're crazy. Sal is here and he brought Betty here to the house and they are o.k." I felt good that Betty and Sal got away. My brother had nothing to do with anything that I was involved in. In an Italian family, we were raised up to always protect the family, by not taking accusation against them without true facts. They put me in a cell with thirty other inmates and my beard grew long and I had no other communication with anyone in the outside world. I had no lawyer or anyone to talk to. While inside I spent most of my time playing cards and singing.

One night there was a hustler, a big and very strong man who came there with his lover. Nobody liked these two homosexuals. They had a sexual relationship right in the cell where there were more than thirty bunks in one room. Several days later, while we were getting our meals through the bars, someone stole my dessert. As I turned around to get my spoon, I noticed my dessert was gone. I shouted, "Who stole my dessert? You better give it back to me or we are going to fight." This big strong man, one of the two homosexuals stood up and said, "I got the cookie. Get up. I want to fight you." As they made a circle I positioned myself to fight this big strong guy. Within two minutes I had him over the bars and gave him three shots in the kidneys and I had the victory over him. The police came over and wanted to find out what happened. They removed me and put me in a solitary cell. I spent 10 days eating nothing but bread and water. After 45 days I looked through the little window of my cell and I saw a man who looked like a District Attorney. I said, "Please help me. I've been here for 45 days." He replied, "What's your name?" I told him my name and I told him how long I had been there. He was like an angel sent from God. One hour later the deputy dismissed me and released me from jail. They gave me a shower and shave and I was sent before a judge. While in front of the judge, the District Attorney told him that I was an innocent victim. They apologized to me and released me and gave me my freedom. They gave me my car back but the police kept the jewelry. Why? For their own selfish purposes. Because if they would have made a case against me, then they had to give up the jewelery. They were not willing to because the jewelry was stolen from people from other countries or other states. There were no witnesses pressing on for their loot. The police kept it all for their own filthy habits and greed.

    I was happy to get my freedom but my soul was scarred and very deeply wounded, because of how they handled the law. I felt they were more corrupt than me. Sure, I stole the jewelry but their job was to report it or restore it back to the owner. Instead they kept it for their own greed. I thought for a moment, where is God in their lives? Sure they carried their shining badge but they were violating the laws, the laws of the land. I felt that this was nothing but a big game. I drove back to New Jersey. My brother Joe and his wife Anna were running a pizza shop. They were married and had three children. He was the most decent of my family. He was a born leader. As the story unfolds I will share more about the miracle of the life of Joe. I crashed there for three or four days and several days later, Sal and Betty were glad to see me. I truly loved my brother. It was Italian tradition that the big brother takes care of the younger brother. Even more so because my father passed away a few years prior. My father made me take a vow to take care of Sal. Here I am now, I got beat up and went to jail for 45 days because the police were looking for him. I'm taking the rap and the beating and he's not even aware of it. I could have been bitter against him and have hatred but I chose not to because he didn't even know what was going on and the police had no case against him. They were just fishing and looking to create something against Sal. Everything ended smooth. I made up in my mind that I would never be poor. I would always be rich and the system was going to pay for it. Regardless, I was going to get what I wanted.

For the next three months I worked in the pizza shop making pizzas and delivering. I remember in the late sixties that a twenty inch pizza was only 80 cents and Joe had five delivery men. I was a substitute. I recall it was early February, there was twenty inches of snow on the ground. It was very hard to drive without the chains. The pizza shop was located in a city called Cliffside Park. There were many hills and down-roads and up-roads. I remember the customers always asked for the pizza to be brought hot. The reward was a five dollar tip. Now as I look back I remember that those were happy days. I would make twenty delivery's a night and about 80 to 100 dollars in tips. I was happy, I was free, and it was fun to rush to the client a hot pie. I always enjoyed pleasing people but somehow without instruction or a mentor in my life and without family structure, Satan lured me back into the big city, he not done with me yet. I was misled. I took the road of unrighteousness.

A FEW HIGHLIGHTS OF SAL

Several years later Sal moved west to California as a carpenter trying to find destiny and identity. He was fortunate that some of his friends pushed him with the Gospel. He heard God's voice and dedicated himself to the Lord with a great recovery from gambling and other substances. Sometime later Sal met his soul mate, a beautiful, wonderful, spirit-filled young lady. A native of California. Sal became a builder, a general contractor, and he moved to Kona, Hawaii and raised up three beautiful children. At the present time he lives in Arizona where he is raising up his family in the way of the Lord. By the way, he's a great preacher and he has a great testimony. I hope that some day you will meet him. Allelujah! The scripture that comes to my mind is:

I John 3:4-9 Everyone who commits sin also breaks the law; sin is the breaking of law. You know that He was revealed so that He might take away sins, and there is no sin in Him. Everyone who remains in Him does not sin; everyone who sins has not seen Him or known Him. Little children, let no one deceive you! The one who does what is right is righteous, just as He is righteous. The one who commits sin is of the devil, for the devil has sinned from the beginning. The Son of God was revealed for this purpose: to destroy the devil's works. Everyone who has been born of God does not sin, because His seed remains in him; he is not able to sin, because he has been born of God.

I wish somebody would have hit me over the head and taught me this when I was a child. But, on the other hand, this book would have been different. It is the way it is so you can relate to it and come to Jesus, to destroy the work of the devil in your life. Amen.

5
A LITTLE FISH IN BIG NEW YORK CITY

I was a strong young man and I was drawn back to the night life of the Big Apple, New York City. There I joined my old buddies. I did not know then what I know now. Somehow the people that were around me, they made me feel good. It was like a negative high. My friends lived a life of debauchery and immorality and there I was again being swallowed up by the big lie of the god of this world, Satan. I felt that I was being rejected by the system and by the community. My identity and my character were darkened by bitterness and resentment. Yet deep inside of me I believed that someday my life would change after I became wealthy. I would give the low life up. I was totally deceived because I disrespected the laws of the land. Because of the surrounding immoral activity and the greed that I saw, it made me believe a lie. So instead of riches and freedom, destruction, pain and deception were ahead of me.

The Bible declares in Proverbs 10:2,
Treasures of wickedness profit nothing: but righteousness delivereth from death.

BAS Translation: "Wealth which cometh from sin is of no profit, but righteousness gives salvation from death."

ATT Translation: "Wealth which comes from sin is of no profit, but righteousness gives salvation from death."

These proverbs are God's laws. When we honor them and respect them the enemy cannot win. I was totally disconnected from God and disobedient to him. My foolishness and my greed gave me a false fame and security. My goal was to make a big score. I wanted to become a better jewel thief and a better gambler so that I could make a lot of money and beat the system. I reasoned that someday I would be a better poker player and be famous and beat the odds. I wanted to be recognized as one of the great ones. I wanted to own a casino in Las Vegas or Monte Carlo.

Several weeks later I found out that Louie Greco was rigging the gambling and robbing the customers by using a professional mechanic. By mixing the cards in a certain way, people would always come out second and not first. If a person was not aware of it, there was no way to find out. Many times you have seen this in a movie or in Las Vegas. Some casinos have been known in the past to rig the table and take wealth from the innocent. Dear reader, be careful that this is not you or your family. When I found out I was being robbed, I confronted them and I asked very politely to give my money back. They denied my request and declared that it was not true, saying, I was just a lousy player. They stated they would war against me and that I better pay all or they would destroy me. At that time I was not a terrorist. I was just a little fish in big New York City and I had no connections. I was not affiliated with the mafia. If anyone is affiliated with the mafia, then they will go to protect you and fight on your behalf and settle things in the wrong way.

Dear reader, remember, I had no faith in the police any longer. Since they beat me up and put me in jail and the attorneys sold me down the river, I was in bad shape. Wouldn't you say so? At other nightclubs that I frequently went to as a night bird, I was advised by my so called mafia friends to get a gun and expect to fight the crooked club owner or run. I never owned or had used a gun before. I knew my life was now at stake and that I was to have a real confrontation. I went out and bought two illegal guns. The next morning, I went to the Hudson River and began to target shoot into the river, to test the guns. At this time

From Mafia Boss to the Cross

in my testimony I would like to define the word Mafia, to express the full meaning of it in the English language.

This is what I found in the Webster's Dictionary:

1. A secret terrorist organization in Sicily, operating in the early 19th century in opposition to legal authority.
2. A secret criminal organization of Italian origin operating in the United States and engaging in illegal activities such as gambling, drug dealing, prostitution, blackmail, extortion, and racketeering.
3. Any of various similar criminal organizations especially when dominated by members of the same nationality
4. Informal tightly knit group of trusted associates as of a political leader.
5. Italian perhaps from dialectical mafia bluster and boldness. Blackmail, racketeering, common Italian immigrants.

The one called Mafioso is a member of the Mafia which becomes separated from liberty, justice, and freedom of the laws of God, country and his fellow man. The life-style is anti-Christ, anti-social, and an eye for an eye and a tooth for a tooth. The image of this mafioso is like the men seen in the movies. Someone like Al Capone. They are perceived as the finer man with the hat, big cigar, fancy suit and a 38 pistol. The man who wants to be boss. In the natural man does not want to respect God's laws or the laws of the land. Mankind has abused his freedom and likes to stand on his own on top of the world. Like the movie, 'Scarface', that came out in the 1980's starring Al Pacino. This is a type of man who is out to kill and destroy and does not have a good character. It seems like in America, since the early 1930's, many people have accepted this false image. We have heard of Irish mafia in Queens, New York and names from the past such as Bugsy Malone and Jewish bootleggers of the Jazz era.

But I remind you that behind this personality and character is nothing but the work of demons. Man is full of pride, deception, and is out to deceive himself and others. The Bible warns us about this character. By the way, dear reader, is this you? Or someone you know? I strongly encourage you to read this book. I believe this book is written especially for you. I have been praying for twenty years that my story may be released into your hands. The Mafia, and all that it stands for, is designed to deceive, control, manipulate and rob innocent people. This did not begin yesterday or a hundred years ago. It began in the garden of Eden. Genesis 3:6: "When Satan, through the serpent, deceived Eve and she ate the fruit." She violated the commandments of God. This is not a racial issue, whether Italian, Irish, Chinese, Black, Russian, Hispanic or Jewish. This is a issue of the violation of the principles of God. Satan tries to defile and disqualify the Bible and what it stands for. God's principles of the supreme law which must be established on the Earth.

The word Mafioso, or Mafia, is translated 'to hurt innocent people'. These immigrants are not law abiding citizens and do not know their rights nor do they respect others rights. I appeal to you: My purpose at this time in my testimony is to give you a foundation of truths about life and to fill you with many thoughts about Biblical theology. This is because the Bible is the ultimate foundation in the courts. The Declaration of Independence, which our forefathers of America: Samuel Adams, Thomas Jefferson, John Adams and Benjamin Franklin wrote in 1776, held to a Biblical standard of freedom, liberty and justice for all. They believed that all men are equal, born to live in the standards of the laws of God. George Washington and other great men fought for our freedoms. These are the principles that made America strong and also the same principles that Satan and the Mafia are trying to destroy. We find that the word Mafia in Hebrew Translation is "of the devil or Satan" and very clearly the Bible states in 1 Corinthians 4:4 that Satan is the god of this world. Satan is working seven days a week, 24 hours a day, not only in America but also around the world, trying to defile the word of God and the laws of God. You and I can see that the Mafia exists within every nationality and race. As you watch movies or travel you find that there are gangs in different levels of society, not only in America, but also around the world.

You also find people full of integrity and honesty who live with good standards and morals. They strive to obey the laws, to live with morality and choose to be the best for their Nation. As I studied American history I discovered that the pilgrims who came to America in addition to Christopher Columbus and Americo Vespucci, were

Christian missionaries. They were the pillars of the faith that made America strong. Now, as we live in the year 2007, we see immorality, dishonesty and perversion are trying to destroy and corrupt everything that America stands for. You and I need to pray that America will return to our God. The one who gave us this great nation.

Here are four points that give the solution to get rid of the problem that exists around the world and gives hope to all humanity.

WHY AM I HERE!

1. GOD MADE ME, TO LOVE ME!
   Jeremiah 31:3
   God says, "I have loved you with an everlasting love!"

   Ephesians 1:4-5
   Long ago, even before he made the world, God loved us and chose us in Christ to be held without fault in his eyes. His unchanging plan has always been to adopt us into his own family by bringing us to himself through Jesus Christ. This gave him great pleasure.

2. WE WERE CREATED TO ENJOY A PERSONAL RELATIONSHIP WITH GOD AND TO MANAGE HIS CREATION! THIS MAKES US SPECIAL!

   Genesis 1:27-28
   So God created people in his own image; God patterned them after himself; Male and female he created them. God blessed them and told them, "Multiply and fill the earth and subdue it. Be masters over the fish and the birds and all the animals.

   1 Timothy 6:17
   But their trust should be in the living God, who richly gives us all we need for our enjoyment.

3. WHEN WE KNOW AND LOVE GOD, AND LIVE IN HARMONY WITH HIS PURPOSE FOR OUR LIVES, IT PRODUCES TREMENDOUS BENEFITS IN OUR LIVES:

a. Clear Conscience (Romans 8:1)
   b. Purpose (Romans 8:28)
   c. Power and Strength (Philippians 4:13)
   d. Life and Peace (Romans 8:6)
   e. Confidence (Romans 8:31)
   f. Fulfillment (Philipians 4:19)
   g. Help with Weakness (Romans 8:26)
   h. Security (Romans 8:39)
   i. Freedom (John 8:32,36)

THIS IS THE KIND OF LIFESTYLE GOD INTENDS FOR US TO LIVE!

Jesus said,

John 10:10
My purpose is to give life in all its fullness.

IF THIS IS TRUE, WHY AREN'T MOST PEOPLE HAPPY? WHAT'S THE PROBLEM?

1. Humanity has a natural desire to BE THE BOSS and to ignore God's principles for living.

This is communicated in our words and lifestyle:

   a. "Look out for #1."
   b. "Do your own thing."
   c. "If it feels good, do it!"
   d. "I want what I want, when I want it"
   e. "Who cares what God has to say about it!"
   f. "It's my life and I'll do what I please!"

THE BIBLE CALLS THIS ATTITUDE SIN.

Sin is a biblical word that means "to miss the mark."
Key word: REBELLION

> Isaiah 53:6
> All of us have strayed away like sheep. We have left God's paths to follow our own.

> 1 John 1:8
> If we say we have no sin, we are only fooling ourselves and refuse to accept the truth.

Sin breaks our close relationship with God. Sin separates us from God and causes us to live our lives outside of His will. But there is a problem -

> Isaiah 59:2
> your sins have cut you off from God.

> Romans 3:23
> All have sinned and fall short of God's glorious standard.

IT LOOKS LIKE THIS...

All the best attempts in the world won't get you to where you need to be. Many people say things like:

  a. "My mother was a Christian so..."
  b. "I'm a really good person."
  c. "I'll give up all my bad habits."
  d. "I'll work real hard and earn it."
  e. "I go to church all the time."

Sin / Death
The result of any attempts to be righteous on our own is worthless. The Bible teaches us that our attempts lead to DEATH. A relationship with God is NOT based on anything you DO.

> Proverbs 16:25 (NIV)
> There is a way that seems right to a man, but in the end it leads to death.

When our relationship with God is not right, it causes PROBLEMS in every area of our lives: friendships, school, parents, jobs, finances, etc.

WHAT'S THE SOLUTION?

Jesus said,

> John 14:6 (NIV)
> I am the way, the truth, and the Life. No one comes to the Father, except through me!

God came to earth as a human being [in Jesus] to bring us back to Himself. If any other way would have worked, Jesus would not have had to come. "The Way" is through the person of Jesus!

> Romans 6:23
> For the wages of sin is death, but the free gift of God is eternal life through Christ Jesus our Lord.

JESUS HAS ALREADY TAKEN CARE OF YOUR SIN PROBLEM WHEN HE DIED ON THE CROSS!

> 1 Timothy 2:5
> For there is only one God and one Mediator who can reconcile God and people. He is the man Christ Jesus.

WHY DID GOD SEND JESUS TO DIE IN YOUR PLACE?

God did this for YOU because He loves YOU and wants YOU TO KNOW Him.

From Mafia Boss to the Cross

Romans 5:8
But God showed his great love for us by sending Christ to die for us while we were still sinners.

God has already done His part to restore our relationship to Him. HE TOOK THE INITIATIVE. NOW HE WAITS FOR EACH OF US to individually ACCEPT what he has done for us.

WHAT DOES GOD WANT ME TO DO?

1. ADMIT THAT GOD HAS NOT BEEN FIRST PLACE IN YOUR LIFE AND ASK HIM TO FORGIVE YOUR SINS.

   1 John 1:9
   But if we confess our sins to him, he is faithful and just to forgive us and to cleanse us from every wrong.

2. BELIEVE THAT JESUS DIED TO PAY FOR YOUR SINS, HE AROSE AGAIN FROM THE GRAVE, AND IS ALIVE TODAY.

   Romans 10:9
   For if you confess with your mouth that Jesus is Lord and believe in your heart that God raised him from the dead, you will be saved.

   Acts 4:12
   There is a salvation in no one else! There is no other name (Jesus) in all heaven for people to call on to save them.

3. ACCEPT GOD'S FREE GIFT OF SALVATION. DON'T TRY TO EARN IT.

   Ephesians 2:8-9
   God saved you by his special favor when you believed. You can't take credit for this; it is a gift from God. Salvation is not a reward for the good things we have done, so none of us can

boast about it. Salvation comes to us from above by the power of the Holy Spirit through Grace, Faith, and Christ alone.

Our relationship with God is not restored by anything we do, but on the basis of what Jesus already did for us!

4. INVITE JESUS CHRIST TO COME INTO YOUR LIFE AND BE THE DIRECTOR ("LORD") OF YOUR LIFE.

John 1:2-13
But to all who believed him and accepted him, he gave the right to become children of God. They are reborn! This is not a physical birth resulting from human passion or plan - this rebirth comes from God.

5. IF YOU BELIEVE YOU BELONG TO HIM.

Romans 10:13
For anyone who calls on the name of the Lord will be saved.

YOU CAN TAKE THESE STEPS BY PRAYING A SIMPLE PRAYER OF COMMITMENT TO GOD.

IT MIGHT BE SOMETHING LIKE THIS...

"Dear Jesus, thank you for making me and loving me, even when I've ignored you and gone my own way. I realize I need you in my life and I'm sorry for my sins. I ask you to forgive me. Thank you for dying on the cross for me. Please help me to understand it more. As much as I know presently, I want to follow you from now on. Please come into my life and fill me with the power of your Holy Spirit and with your precious blood that was shed on the cross. Write my name in Heaven in the Book of the Lamb and cleanse me and remove my evil character and give me your Holy Spirit to make me the person that you want me to be. From this day forward I will read the Bible and proclaim you to be the only Lord, King, and God in my life. In Jesus' name, AMEN.

Congratulations! Now that you've made this important decision, tell someone. If you would like to, contact us through our email, or come to our location. We would be more than happy to assist you, pray with you and help you on your journey to discover the great calling that God has for your life. Amen.

6
EXPOSING THE DECEPTION AND CONTROL OF THE MAFIA

There are five powerful families who control all the East Coast from New York City to the border of Canada and from New Jersey all the way to Sacramento, on the west coast in California. There are different levels of Mafia Boss. Remember, it's like an army structure. You have the soldier, the sergeant, the corporal and you have the generals. These five families build their position through violence. As I continue the journey of my testimony I remind you, this is part of my dark past, prior to coming to Christ. It is not easy for me to look back and remember the demonic, horrible stories. I will remind you that in this book I will be specific in the details, revealing my conversion - how I came to Christ. It was very dramatic and I believe you will find this to be an exciting story. Now, let us continue with some highlights of my life in the fast lane, on the road of unrighteousness. I remind you that I was a young man with no instructions, moral compass or faith.

Due to past experiences, I felt that the police in New York City were corrupt. I did not see any goodness in the social life that I lived in the clubs amidst all the nightlife. People discussed how the police would take bribes. Despite my evil character, I knew that this was totally wrong. As the nights went on, I associated with gamblers, club people and individuals who owned jewelry stores and who were prominent in the garment industry. Some of them were bookmakers and the majority of them gambled on football, horses, baseball and others. The clubs that I associated with were located in downtown Manhattan, Uptown Manhattan, East side, Westside, Brooklyn, Long Island and New Jersey. All these clubs and gambling houses were called 'goulash joints'. This is a nickname for an association or a recreational club.

My life was spent gambling. I became addicted to gambling and I began to dream about gambling. I meditated about gambling. I lost a majority of time. I read books about gambling and I wanted to be the best. My dream was to go to Vegas someday and build a casino. This was because many of the people I associated with in the late 50's and in the 60's promoted themselves there. Some of you may have watched some gangster movies like Al Capone or the Godfather. As you watched it you might have thought that it was a good movie. Well these were real facts. The Italians, the Irish and the Jews were fighting for territorial control in illegal gambling because of the black market profits of hundreds of billions of dollars annually. At this point, I want to make a clear statement concerning the Mafia. In my story I will not give out any names to protect my fellow man. Some of the names in this book have been changed. In New York City there are five families that have, since 1918, oppressed innocent people. Some of them are so deeply involved that the only way out for them is to die and go to hell. The other route is to be a miracle, like me, and come to Jesus Christ (because the Bible says all wrong is sin). 1 John 5:17 says: All unrighteousness is sin and there is a sin not unto death.

You see, this is not religion. These are spiritual facts concerning life and they are truths. God's laws are truths but unfortunately we have an enemy (the devil) who controls people's minds and provokes people to do wrong. Many of these people are leaders in positions of power. Many came to this wonderful country America, a place of opportunity, and have taken the wrong road. It's very clear that the people in authority in the government are ordained by God to do right and to punish all evil. The civic leaders and police are to be honest and act with integrity and the government and the police are ordained by God to do right and to punish all evil and to be honest and act with integrity.

Unfortunately the people I associated with did not have good personalities or moral character. As a matter of fact, as I recollect, the majority of the people I knew worshipped the Mafia. These people liked the fame and life in the fast lane. God will and does bless people who do honest work and perform transactions with integrity. But I saw myself get caught up in the exciting action of the fast lanes of New York City. I continued in this lifestyle. I was sleeping in the daytime and gambling at night. I remember living in a hotel room, which I rented weekly.

In early 1966 I met Angela while in a nightclub dancing. Sweet Angela was seventeen years old, 5'4", with a beautiful body and gorgeous hair. She looked like Sophia Loren. After dancing with her that night we exchanged phone numbers. The following day at 3pm she called me. The first thing she said was, "Bruno come and get me. Someone is beating me up". She sounded desperate, she was crying and in a lot of pain. I met her 21 minutes later at her location. She was holding her rib area and crying. She told me that a pimp had beat her and took her money. So I took my gun and went to go see him. I met with this 27 year old man named Anthony. I had a serious conversation with him. He told me that she was his girl. The conversation turned violent and we got into a fist-fight. He busted my nose and I busted his mouth. I warned him to stay away from her. Beautiful Angela became my partner, lover, and room-mate.

Several weeks later we got a one bedroom apartment on 96th street in Westside Manhattan. We lived together. Night after night we would go out to eat at the fanciest and most expensive restaurant in New York City called the, 'Monsignor'. This restaurant was located on 53rd and Madison. This restaurant became very famous because Anastasia, an illustriously famous gangster, was gunned down inside the restaurant. The owner was a small-time Mafioso. The 'Monsignor' restaurant was where the movie stars, royalty (kings and princes), and governors would associate. The owner, Salvatore, and his brother Giovanni were notorious gamblers and very well know in the community and among mobsters.

Several months had gone by and one night I got a phone call from a mafia soldier named Louie Greco. He was the one I owed $15,000 to. They asked for the money. I replied that I would not pay. The following day at about 7 at night they got behind my car, tailed me and signaled me to pull over. They were waving their guns. Angela was with me and the chase began. After about one hour of chasing me through the city I began to feel both excitement and trauma. My blood pressure was high. I felt that Satan was engaging me in spiritual warfare. I managed to get away from them. The following day at two in the afternoon, as I was returning to my apartment, I saw about 60 feet away from me two gangsters running towards me. I took a 38 special, cranked it, and shot one shot in the air. I said, "If you guys don't get out of here, you're going to get it". They ignored my warning and fought back. I hid behind a wall and I could feel the breeze of the bullet and chills went through my spine. I began to sweat. In my mind I was thinking, "These dirty bastards. They got the nerve to come to my house. They ripped me off and now they are trying to kill me." Hate came to my heart and I had a desire to kill both of them. I moved my position and got behind the car on the street. They took another two shots at me and were coming towards me. I shot back four shots and this caused cars to move onto the sidewalk. People were screaming. Within a few seconds, the police were on their way. Richie C. and his friend ran. I was happy to see that. Now realizing the police would be there in a few seconds, I ran to my building on the tenth floor and dumped the guns in the incinerator.

Within a few minutes there were police everywhere on the street. When I got to my apartment on the sixth floor the police came to my door saying, "Are you okay." I said, "Yeah, I'm ok." They asked me, "Where are your guns?" I replied, "I don't have any guns." They quickly searched my apartment and asked me to go downstairs. They began to interrogate me. There was a black man pointing to me and he identified me as one of the participants in the shoot-out. I looked at the black man and said, "You're mistaken, and if it was me I am going to come out and get you." He told the police, "No, it's not the guy." The police let me go. They said to me, "Are you in trouble with the mafia?" I said, "No, I'm ok". Well, within several days of this incident, it became known at every club in New York City. The top Mafioso began to investigate of me. After hearing so many things about me, they made a decision to promote me to a wise guy. How they promote you is, they give you a territory and you become one of the victims. They give you a position in the organization and a location. For example: being in control of the lottery. Some people get involved in the book-making, some in operating nightclubs, and many other things. My reply was "No, Thank you." Down deep in my heart not only did I not like who I was or what I did, but I knew that someday I would be out of it. I made a decision and took a vow to myself that I would never be poor. I wanted to be rich because I felt that money was power. I knew I could get people out of jail. I knew I could bribe people, but money could buy anything. That was my concept. The Bible, on the other hand, is contrary to this. Proverbs says, "Do not seek to be rich too fast. It leads to evil." And yet I did not want to be in the Mafia and be controlled by anyone. I did not really like their works. People are peculiar, even today in 2007, there are people not only in New York City but also around the world controlling illegal activity by Mafia associations.

Several months passed by and Richie C. and Tommy 'the hat' both were killed in terrible violence. Richie C. was a hit man for the mafia. One day, in a fist fight, he struggled with a man and during the struggle the gun pointed towards his stomach and went off and killed him. Tommy 'the hat' was shot by the mafia sixty times. In downtown New York City, there is an area called 'Little Italy' where all the retired wise guys associated, in a goulash joint. A New York Times article declared that Tommy C. took a machine gun and went to kill all the people in the nightclub because he was sent there by another mafia family. As he entered the club and pulled the trigger the machine gun jammed. He fled for his life and the owners of the club, within twenty four hours, took vengeance in upstate New York. He was found with sixty bullets in his chest.

Angela was living with me and she was 18 years old now. She was adopted from Italy when she was 12 years old as an orphan. We lived together for five years and then we got married. Angela was a victim just like me. I know now what I didn't know then. She was adopted by an American family in Long Island. Within several weeks of her arrival from Italy, the man that adopted her began to sexually abuse her, to the point where she ran away from home. Angela looked like a movie star. Her face was like an Angel. She became my crime partner. I never knew about a personal relationship with the family that adopted her. She never told me. If she were to tell me, I would have settled the situation my own way. She kept it very personal, to herself, for many years.

As the days passed I worked in a nightclub.

My addiction to gambling became worse. Not only am I playing cards, but I was gambling horses, even football. Disaster struck again. Here is what the people were doing in the nightclubs. Even though it is illegal in New York City to own a private gambling house, the customers would buy chips so that there was no money on the tables. If they played poker, the house would take 5% of every pot. It made no difference whether it was blackjack, poker or card games. They would sometimes go on for 24 hours in a day. They would have regular dealers taking shifts and cocktail waitresses providing drinks and food. I remember that some people would go on a gambling bash for seven days in a row. I remember watching family and business associates loose everything. My crime partner, Ricky, was also a gambler. He was my provoker and my mentor in jewel thieving. One day we decided to go to Vegas. He told me he had connections in Vegas. So in 1969 we went. We drank a-lot and we had a good time. We met some underground people who had master keys to the best hotels in Las Vegas. Ricky was notorious and liked to talk a lot. After one successful robbery we continued robbing more jewelry. Then the police got on our tail and we were arrested. While in jail, through a mafia connection, I managed to call Angela in New York. We got a lawyer in Vegas who had a connection with the sheriff. He told us that for $10,000 we could walk. Angela managed to get the money and we were released of seven burglary charges and over $150,000 in stolen jewelry. The police kept all the jewelry and we were free. I learned that day that Las Vegas was very corrupt.

We went back to New York City. Because of many years spent gambling, and my experience, I came to a conclusion that I would open my own nightclub. On 23rd street and 10th avenue in downtown New York City I opened up a restaurant with the intention of running illegal card games. Several months later after much investment my partner, who was supposed to be the chef, went to the hospital with a double-hernia. Consequently the restaurant was not successful. I began to invite other gamblers that I knew and for several weeks we had a sociable card game operating. After only 30 days the Mafia came to visit me. I was told that they wanted to have a little talk with me.

While meeting them, they made it clear to me that this was their territory. They told me I could not operate there unless I gave them 20% of the profits. I replied, "I'm not bothering anyone. I'm just having some fun here." They told me, "We wanted you to join us and you refused. Now you are trying to be your own boss and this is our territory." They told me to either pay 20% or they would burn the place down. Or the police would bust the place. Well, several weeks went by and the police came in and arrested everyone. What I found out was that the police in New York City, the undercover police, their job was to close any gambling operation unless it was protected and paid by the Mafia.

The Mafia was paying the police to keep the nightclubs open. The place was shut down. Several days later, I met a Jewish fellow named Tommy. He was a small-time crook. His reputation was to use stolen credit cards to buy airline tickets. This man was notorious and everybody knew him. The mafia had connections in the bank. A lady employee provided them with credit card numbers. Tommy would go out and buy thousands and thousands of airline tickets using those credit card numbers. Tommy was also a gambler who had a very bad record with the police. One morning, his wife called me and told me that Tommy was arrested and that he was at the police station. That he wanted me to get him out. I was very well dressed. That was one thing I learned as a jewel thief. One of my mentors in those days who was on a program on television called, "It takes a thief", was Robert Wagner. He was a famous jewel thief on this program and he could open up doors, locks, anything. So, I had this fantasy to become a famous jewel thief. To rob from the rich and give to the poor. This was a lie from Satan. He had put it in my mind.

That morning I got dressed and went to the police station. When I walked inside there were over hundred police. The Chief of Police came out. I remember that it was early February and the weather was very cold. The Chief of Police was drinking wine and he looked at me and said, "Can I help you?" I replied, "I'm looking for Tommy." He pointed and said, "There he is". Tommy was handcuffed to a radiator heater. He said to me, "What do you want with him?" I said, "He's my nephew. I want to help him." He said, "What do you want with him? He's a thief and a junkie." I said, "He's my nephew". The Chief of Police said, "No, you look like a lawyer. You can't be related to this scum of the earth". Silently, the Chief of Police said, "He has terrorized the city all night long. He was chased from the police trying to rob the Prime Ministers' wife and my men have been chasing him all night long. He is facing twenty years. Then he turned around toward me and said, "Do you want to get him out?" He said to me, "$30,000". Wow, I was stunned. This little Irishmen in his sixties was now bribing me. He said, "He has not been booked yet, I can change the papers." I said to him, "I can

From Mafia Boss to the Cross

give you $15,000" he turned around and said, "20." I shook his hand and went to my back pocket and gave him $10,000 and said, "When he comes out, I will give you the other 10". He gave me a glass of wine and we had a verbal agreement. At 11am that morning Tommy was released. His wife gave me $40,000. I paid the $20,000 and I made a profit of $20,000 for myself. I had a connection with the Chief of Police so when some of the nightclubs in New York City were being busted by the undercover police, I began to take over. I became a more notorious leader and gambler. I still had the urge, desire and addiction to be a jewel thief. I had available to me, keys to the nicest hotels in New York City. My life was not working. I had known much affliction and darkness in my life already. But still there was a sense and feeling of excitement in the nightlife. In the adventures that I was getting into.

Night after night, the Monsignor restaurant would be a place for me to go and escape. The music, the violin, the prestige and the wonderful dinner there were all familiar. The owner would always find a millionaire who liked to drink and play blackjack. From time to time, after the restaurant closed, we would find someone who was drinking with beautiful, prestigious women. The owner would invite me to participate in these private card games and he would set up a mechanic against these millionaires. Before the night was over we would end up with our share of between $30-50,000. But money would never last; we would take some from one place and loose it at another place. The addiction would get stronger and stronger. Two or three times a year we would go to Vegas or Florida to target some hotel millionaires. We did this for several years. It was a lifestyle but the law was against us. From time to time we would get arrested and booked for burglary and breaking and entering. Most of the time, being that these were public hotels, the charge would only be a misdemeanor and not a felony. I found a Jewish lawyer. We will call him John. He would always fight for us even though we were guilty. Somehow we would manage to pay off the clerk in the court buildings or manage to get favor with a judge by giving him money or gifts. Sometimes with a car or diamond watch. Always, the lawyer managed for us to stay out of jail. Sometimes, at big sexual parties, other beautiful woman would visit the judge in sexual encounters so that we could obtain more favor with the judge. This went on for many years. Ricky DiAngelo, my mentor as a jewel thief, was more aggressive in illegal activities. I even despised him and many times I despised myself for being evil minded. But yet I felt in my heart that someday this would stop. In reality I found myself getting deeper and deeper. After having money in my hand, we would go into gambling houses and money would disappear. I know now that I did not take responsibility for my mistakes and I allowed the lies of the god of this world to allure me deeper and deeper into my prison.

As I dealt with the problems of my arrests I began to discover that the system was corrupt. That they would take bribes and the charges would be dismissed or reduced. Dear Reader, this was a real jungle. None of us had the fear of God. We were getting deeper in immorality and debauchery of all sorts. We would get in trouble because we were jewel thieves and we were taking jewelry from the tourists in the hotels. There were never really any people involved in eyewitness accounts and most of the time the people would go back to their own country. They almost never had the time to show up in court to testify. This was one advantage that we had. The more we got away from going to jail, the easier it was for us to do more wrong. Meanwhile the years kept going by. The police in New York City knew about our activities and though most of the police were corrupt, some were not. Some did their duty and I thank God for them. We knew our limitations and being that there was corruption in the system, we took advantage of the situation. Some of the police had personal vendettas against me. When I found this out, fear got a hold of me and I thought, I better cool it! One afternoon in a barbershop we met with other underground jewel thieves. Merf the Surf was there. He was the number one jewel thief in the world in the 1960's. He pulled off one of the largest jewel heists known in those days. He stole the magnificent 'Star of India' diamond. By the way, he was also touched by the Lord and has been for quite some time, a born again Christian. He wrote a book called "Jewels for Christ." At the present time God is using him mightily around the world to share his testimony. Hallelujiah!

That day, in the barber shop, Merf told me that I had better cool it. He advised me to go to a Puerto Rican island resort. He gave me some of his contacts. The following day I was on a plane to Puerto Rico. There a made some undercover contacts and was quickly back in the game of jewel thieving. In Puerto Rico there are many resorts and very wealthy people from all over the world go there. It is the second Monte Carlo. Movie stars, professional gamblers, and even mobsters went to this island. Puerto Ricans are a high class mafia. While there I spent weeks at a time, swimming, scuba diving, dancing and gambling. I met women from all over the world. At the planned time I stole world class precious jewels through working with an inside connection. Then I fled back to the States. When the undercover police in New York City, through their informers heard I went to Puerto Rico, they pursued me. Here is the story as close as I can remember. My connections in Puerto Rico informed me that there were tourists renting a small yacht. They were descendents of the Queen of Sheba. Through my contact I learned that they were carrying two million dollars worth of jewelry that night.

Immediately I worked out my strategy, a plan to carefully steal these precious jewels. The yacht was parked on a side bay. At three o'clock sharp in the afternoon I was to go there and get the safe. I could not make any noise to alert them of my presence. I was told that there was a safe that was portable. It weighed about 120 pounds. I rented a small motorboat, approached the targeted yacht and scuba-dived to the boat. When I climbed into the boat I managed to get to the safe but I was not able to open it. I picked up the heavy safe and threw it overboard, into the water. It was maybe fifteen feet deep. Then I swam under water, picked up the safe and carried it as if it were a toy to my boat. As a boy I learned this trick. When I was ten years old in Italy I lived in a resort area. I would tell the tourists that I could walk under the water but they would never believe me. I would ask them, "If I could do this, would you give me a dollar?" They would say "Yes." My trick was that I had a thirty pound rock under fifteen feet of water. From the diving board I would jump, swim under water and catch the rock. I would then walk fifteen or twenty feet under the water. Then I would let go of the rock and quickly swim above. The Navy sailors would applaud me and give me a dollar. Later I would tell them about my trick. In the natural no man can walk under water because the bodies' buoyancy and the currents would lift him up. When I held onto the weight of the rock, although it was thirty pounds, it seemed like ten pounds.

Back to my jewel heist in Puerto Rico. When I got to my boat I tied the safe with a rope. Single handedly I tried to get it on board the boat. However, once it came out of the water the weight was too heavy for me to get it on board. So my only solution was to drag it to shore under water. At that time I was 27 years old. I was strong, because I always worked out. I could swim like a shark. I managed to go to a safe location and some underground connections and I peeled the safe. It was a jackpot. There was nothing in it but jewels and lots of money. That night I checked out of the hotel planning to take a late night flight to the mainland. I hid all the jewelry in the trunk of the car. My hangout was one of my favorite restaurants and casino called "La Concha". There I had a great influence with everyone. People knew me as a great Don Juan, millionaire, and as a mover in the town. My plans were about to change. As the fun began to heat up, the New York City F.B.I were hot on my tail. They knew what I liked and had planned to trap me. Right after dinner I went into the dancehall. There I met two beautiful under cover federal agents who claimed to be tourists. I found out later that they were looking for me for three days. They sweetly smiled at me and I asked them to dance. They claimed they were there vacationing. It is very common in Puerto Rico for people to leave the dance floor and go straight to the casino. I began to play blackjack with these two beautiful ladies next to me, who by now were both loving me and enjoying it. Within forty-five minutes I went from twenty five dollar bets up to thousand dollar bets. Within a matter of thirty minutes I lost all my cash which was more than thirty five thousand dollars. I looked at the watch and suddenly I realized that I had thirty minutes to catch the flight. The ladies smiled and said "Why don't you take an earlier flight tomorrow and stay with us tonight, so we can have some fun." I missed the flight and we went back to dancing. At 12:30 in the morning I drove them to their hotel hoping that we would have a party instead. Instead they gave me the couch in their suite to sleep on. I was given a drink and crashed instantly.

The next thing I knew, it was 6:30 in the morning. The room was full of police and I awakened to see badges and guns at my head. Immediately they read me my rights and handcuffed me. They took me downstairs, and they asked me, "Is that your car?" I replied, 'No!!" One of the undercover woman, replied, "Yes this is your car. We were driving with you." I replied again, "No, this is not my car." They detained me for about thirty minutes because they were operating illegally. They

From Mafia Boss to the Cross

were from New York City and they had no jurisdiction to arrest me. They kept me there so they could get the local police to make an arrest. Meanwhile, they stripped the car and they found all the stolen jewelry. The Puerto Rican authorities told them, "We cannot arrest this man. We have no evidence against him." The agents were frustrated, screaming, "This guy is a bandit, a jewel thief. We have to stop him." They even called the newspapers, to take pictures of me.

During this time my soul and mind were going through so much trauma. I wished for one solitary moment that I was never born. Shame, humiliation, and frustration came upon me. The people in the hotel respected me and they never expected that I was an imposter. That I was a notorious jewel thief. That I was number three in the nation, behind Merf the Surf. Meanwhile, the F.B.I. took me to the local police station to be charged with the crime of burglary. The District Attorney and Chief of Police refused to book me in spite of those allegations. Even the rental car was in a different name. They had nothing on me. But the truth is the truth. For three days they drove more than ninety miles, trying to find a judge to book me. They finally found an old, retired judge who would book me. During these three days they put me in a cage and from time to time they would beat me, question me and call me every name in the book. They would ask me questions such as, "Who are your connections? Where did you get this jewelry from? Who are you working with?" Within 72 hours, they had me tied up to a giant bird cage hanging off the floor like I was a monkey. Believe me, I felt like a monkey!

They gave me no food. A strange thing happened, every hour there were men and women coming in looking to make identification. The majority of these people, they were the victims of a robbery. No one, not one witness signed papers against me. They transported me to the worst jail in the world. It was called Santa Margarita. This jail was worse than the Tijuana jail. They released me into this big room with more than sixty men. Little did I know, everyone of them was in for murder. Immediately after arriving I crashed into a deep sleep because, for three days, I had no sleep. My body was wounded from pain. My nose was broken, two teeth were loose in my mouth and I had fractured ribs. Several hours went by and I was awakened by a drum noise. I looked up and saw that many Puerto Rican inmates were dancing, shouting. I

43

looked down the bunk and noticed that my sandals were missing. Now I am without no shoes. I told the next inmate, "Hey do you know who took my shoes?" His response was, "No but whoever took them, they're not here anymore. They're in a different cell block." So for two days I walked bare footed. Around noon, lunch time, you had to be in line outside the yard where they served rice and beans. If an inmate did not get there in time, he didn't eat.

This event happened in 1968. There in the jail at that time was The 'French Connection', a notorious group of drug dealers. On the third day I lined up for food and I noticed there was an inmate. He was standing, casually reading a magazine with my sandals on his feet. I shouted at him, "Hey, those are my sandals, give them back to me." He backed off in a fight position and whipped out a blade. Within several seconds everybody made a circle around us and he shouted, "I'm 'gonna kill you ,you white man." I removed my shirt and wrapped it around my hand. I tried to nab the knife from his hand. His knife entered my shirt and cut my thumb one inch deep. I quickly gave him two devastating blows, one in the face and one in the chest. He went out like light. Suddenly, the Chief of police shot a machine gun into the air. Everything and everyone came to a halt. He walked up to me and said, "What's going on here?" He looked at me eyeball to eyeball. I looked at him then lowered my eyes towards my sandals. The Chief of police said, "I understand, follow me." I followed him to his office and he gave me a cigarette. He said to me, "I cannot get your sandals back but them guys, they're all murderers, and he belongs to the French Connection." He replied, "I'll do you a favor, I'll get you a new pair of shoes." He walked me into a square circle where there were inmates asleep. He managed to get me a pair of sneakers that were one size too small.

The Chief of Police said to me, "If you have money or jewelry I'll get you out." I told him that if he would make a phone call for me that I would give him 500 dollars. Several days later, he finally contacted my attorney John. Twenty one days later, I was released. John, my lawyer, worked with a local Puerto Rican lawyer and I was set to go to trial. Four months later, the night before trial, while having dinner and discussing the case the Puerto Rican lawyer (we'll call him Ricky) looked at my diamond gold watch. He said to me, "I would like to have a watch like this." I replied, "If you get this case dismissed, not only will I give you this watch, but I'll give you ten-thousand dollars." The very next day we appeared before a female judge. The court room was full of women because the newspapers, that day, put an article: 'Famous jewel thief.' Hundreds of women came to court to check me out. Within fifteen minutes the judge dismissed the case. His ruling was that they had no grounds. Illegal search and seizure and, therefore, no case. That afternoon we went back to the hotel and enjoyed a swim in the pool. At 3:00 Ricky came shouting at us, "I 'gotta get you off this island. The F.B.I. are trying to get a warrant to arrest you again." In desperation we got into a car, then a boat, to get to the States. I arrived in New York City and I never found out what happened to the jewelry. But I'm sure you can take a guess at what happened. I think you are catching on. You and I can suppose that the police kept it all. Or maybe they made some restoration. We will never really know.

Sometime later I went to see my Chief of Police connection. With much convincing he managed to have the undercover cops off my back. I hope as you read my story, that you will not try to do what I did. If you are involved in illegal activity, I promise you that you will be destroyed, you will not win. Because God is watching you and he desires a different plan for your life. So, don't be fools. This story is written to remind someone that crime doesn't pay. The scripture that comes to my mind is:

Jeremiah 4:22
For my people are foolish. They have not known me; They are senseless children and they have no understanding. They are wise to do evil, but to do good, they have no knowledge.

Does this sound like you or part of the environment of people that surround you? I hope not. But this was me. We were wise to do evil, especially coming from another country and living in a city like New York. There the nightlife, in the fast lane without a dream or purpose, can cause sin to take hold of you.

Now that I look back I see that the enemy put a wall around my heart. I thought that there was no justice, but now I know better. God has opened up my eyes to see there are many good people in America. We have a good system, and there are many decent people who believe in liberty, freedom, and justice. As a matter of fact, I can say that we have the best laws in the world in America. God was allowing me to go to jail to get my attention. I was not listening then because rebellion and deception were in my heart. Our fore-fathers fought for our freedom. In the time of Thomas Jefferson in 1778, when they wrote the constitution, it was based on the knowledge of the Bible. The God of the Bible gave us laws. I often pray that this book will be a eye opener for you. Even though Satan got his filthy hands on my life, and was taking me deep into the pit, God remembered me and redeemed me with his love. In the following chapters I will discuss more details of my life, and also my salvation story.

7
YOU DO THE CRIME, YOU DO THE TIME

After the encounter with the Chief of Police bribing me, and getting my friend out of jail, I built an understanding with the Chief of Police. They gave me some power which I know now was a false power. He mentioned to me that anytime I had any problem in the city and needed a favor, I could go to him. One of the ways the mafia worked was to raise up a young man who would go through police academy and became a police officer. However, he was supported and sponsored by the mafia. He was the man inside the system. This is very real and happens even today. The mafia, 'La Famiglia', would always train their family in illegal activities concerning government affairs. On the outside, you think that they are very legal and honest, but yet underground they were corrupted to the core. One day I took inventory of my life. I was getting tired of stealing and selling jewelry, and losing my money to the mafia by gambling. As time went by there were many places in Manhattan, from downtown to uptown, where the club owners were Greeks, Italians, and Jews. When they found out that I had protection and a connection with the police, they all came under my protection. Every one of them became underground in my nightclubs, where I would have 49% of the take. The money began to come in and month after month I would pay the police. At any time if we were late in payment the police would bust us. The restriction the police gave me was that it had to be a social club, with no drugs and no prostitution. Just simple card games. I became more notorious and respected in my circle of illegal activities.

I remember one day I was invited to go to Hoboking, New Jersey. It was the city where Frank Sinatra was born. Some Greeks were running card games in a club. I remember that it was about 7:30pm and I was driving into a very remote area dominated by Puerto Ricans and other Spanish people. I found the club and as I entered it, I was greeted by the owner. A few moments later there was a knock on the door, and when we opened the door, I saw the Puerto Rican Mafia. Joe, the owner, looked through the door hole. He said to us, "The Puerto Rican Mafia is outside." I mentioned to him that I would go outside and talk to them. Everyone looked scared. There were about 20 people in there and I panicked. He opened the door and I went out and he shut the door behind me. I looked at a couple of the mafia leaders. They all had bandanas on their forehead. I asked, "What's going on? What do you want?" One of the guys said, "We want $1000 to give protection." I remember saying, "No way". As they made a circle around me they had knives and bats. Suddenly one of the guys in the back grabs my head and took down a seven inch knife to stab me. I grabbed his arm, flipped him over, and punched him. Another mobster hit me with a bat and one of the guys with a stiletto knife stabbed me in the stomach. I was wounded below my heart and I was struggling and fighting. I chased them. They all fled. I knocked on the door of the club and said, "They all left. Let me in." As they opened the door, they all had fear in their eyes; every single person in the nightclub, both Joe, the owner of the club, and 20 Hungarians, who were in the club. In my heart I was very upset because I felt that I was fighting a fight that did not belong to me. I felt that the people were chickens and cowards by shutting the door behind me. I fell on the couch and I was bleeding. Blood and water were coming out of my stomach. I passed out with no strength.

I woke up in the emergency room. The police informed me that I was scheduled for surgery because I was bleeding internally.

The Chief of Police came in screaming and hollering at me wanting to know what happened and who was involved. He wanted to avenge my stabbing. I replied that this was my first time in the area and that I did not know who did this to me. In surgery they cut me from below my ribs to my lower abdomen. The doctor said I had a close call. For three months, I was on bed rest. The doctor said that I might not be able to walk normally again. I began to go through therapeutic exercises in a gym. In three months I was restored. Angelina was the only one on my side. Even the people in the club never came to visit me. Like the old proverb: "When you got money you got many friends." When you suffer and are poor, there is no one there to support you." I often wondered, "Who am I? Where am I going?" I was still in darkness. I did not believe in demons or the devil and I would do what ever came to my mind. I believed in myself. After four months of agony and pain and through much exercise and determination, I was totally restored. Did I learn my lesson? No. Proverbs declares, the dog goes back to the vomit and a person without knowledge becomes a fool. So I went back to the fast lane.

1969 ENCOUNTER WITH A CARDINAL IN ROME

One night one of the informers, a hotel clerk and one of the gamblers at the clubs, sold us a master key. One of the principles that I lived by was never to rob a home. Only hotels. I was told this by other jewel thieves. That it was an easy target and the punishment was much less. After obtaining the master key, we discovered after 6:30am it was considered daylight. That meant that if we were to get caught, the charge would be much less. We made a rule that we would never steal by breaking and entering while people were sleeping. So one morning, as I was heading to a Hilton in New York City, I went into one of the Royal Suites. In one of the rooms I found a ring which was 3 inches wide and 3 inches long. It had the Pope's signature. I took the ring and sold it to a jewelry store, my connection. Several nights later, at about 11pm, two F.B.I. agents in undercover clothing came to my club. They showed me the picture of the ring. They said, "This ring belongs to a Cardinal and there are 50 F.B.I. agents assigned to the job to recover the ring". The majority of the undercover police were devoted Catholics and they were out to get the ring because they had a lot of respect for their religion. I asked them, "Why did you come to me?" His reply was, "Because you are more connected with the jewelers. You have a better chance of getting it for us. The jewelry store owners are afraid of us because we are the police."

They told me there was a $2,000 reward and they said that they would give me a favor. Anything I wanted, if I were to ever get into trouble. They left me a sketch of the ring. I said, "I will do what I can." God works in strange ways. The following day I went to my fence man, Harry. I said, "Harry, I need this ring back." He replied, "No, no, no, I melted it. I don't have it anymore." I took my gun and cocked it and said, "Harry, don't lie to me. I want the ring back or I will blow your brains out." I reminded him that there were 50 F.B.I. agents shaking the city and the heat was on. I wanted the ring for the best of all of us. Harry said, "Wait a minute." He opened up the safe and there was the ring. I looked at the ring. I put the ring in my hand, and I realized the sentimental value. It was a beautiful 4 ounce ring. I went back to my club and called the undercover police and I showed them the ring. His eyes lit up and he said, "We are very proud of you. Anytime you are in trouble, we owe you one. Tomorrow we are going to give you a $2,000 reward." My response was, "No, you keep the $2,000. I am more than happy to do a good deed." In my heart I felt happier that the pressure was off.

Now I am becoming notorious and I am getting deeper into the crime life. Living with Angela, we decided to finally get married. Several days later the undercover police called me. They said, "The Cardinal is so happy. He wants to meet you and he wants to bless you." The following day we go to midtown, 5th avenue, to the St. Patricks Cathedral. This was one of the most famous Catholic Churches in New York City. Angela and I went to visit the Cardinal and the Cardinal received me. I went into his chambers. I kneeled down and kissed his hand and his ring. He thanked me for finding his ring. Despite my evil works, I felt conviction and I felt God in my life. We mentioned to him that we wanted to get married. He responded, "I will extend my departure and I will stay here and marry you." Two weeks later we contacted all our families. Angela's side lived in Long Island. All her relatives were police officers. On my side was all my immediate family and the rest of the guests were people who I frequented with in the nightlife. At Saint Patrick's Cathedral we had a Royal Wedding. The Cardinal shared a long speech and Angela and I were married. We had the reception at the 'Monsignor'. After the honeymoon I took inventory of my life. I had some cases pending and I was hoping that I would not go to jail. The lawyer informed me that I was becoming notorious and that I probably would be going to jail for three years. We postponed the case time after time. To try to buy some more time so that the heat would be called off. During this time my friend Tommy with the airline ticket scam got into trouble again. I inquired about the situation, he was out on bail but facing 200 years. The judge said he was going to throw the book at him and that he was schizophrenic and a danger to society. They wanted to put him away for good. I went to see my connection, the Chief of Police. He contacted the judge. They said, "The only way he will come out is if you pay $50,000 and a brand new Cadillac." Tommy came up with the $50,000. Then they got a guy who was a car thief to steal a brand new Cadillac. He paid $500 to the thief, and they changed the serial number on the car. At that time, 1970, the mafia had ways to do this. Tommy took the $50,000 and took a brand new Cadillac and sent them to the judge. Several days later I found out that the judge was smoking a cigar and driving a stolen Cadillac. By the way, who is going to suspect a judge of stealing cars? And who was going to give him a ticket for driving a stolen car? In the end, Tommy got 5 years probation and was released.

8
BEATEN AND TORTURED IN LAS VEGAS

When I became a married man I felt that I wanted to do something different with my life. I needed money to try to buy my way out of jail. Ricky DiAngelo approached me with two airline tickets and we went to Las Vegas. It was late 1972. We arrived in Vegas and checked into a small hotel. We gambled and drank all night long. On the second day the police caught me because there were some big robberies happening in the hotels. I was not the only jewel thief. Even 'Merf the Surf' was there and he was very notorious. The police apprehended me and took me to the security office. They began to question me and torture me. They wanted to know who my partners were and who I was working with. I replied that I was by myself and that I didn't do anything wrong. They sprayed mace into my eyes and began to punch me until I fell to the ground. Several hours later a 75 year old man came to see me. He identified himself as Mr. Hilton. He said, "My name is Mr. Hilton and this is my wife Zsa Zsa Gabor." His wife looked at me with an elegant smile and said to me, "Why do you want to be a jewel thief, why don't you be a movie star. You are good looking and you are Italian."

I remember that very moment feeling like dirt. Mental and physical pain was racking my body from the blows. I felt unworthy and now this precious woman was encouraging me to be an actor. In my mind I always thought that the movie stars were a bunch of phonies and that

I was the real actor. I was living a life of pain and agony, and struggles. I looked at her. She was dolled up with a 25 karat diamond ring on her finger. I said to myself, "This lady, she's a Cinderella, how does she know what I have gone through in my life?" The husband replied in a very gentle but firm tone, "These are my hotels." He said in a slow speech, "This is my hotel and I don't want you ever to come back here." He went on saying, "I was told you were here before. I am going to give you a break and let you go but if I find you back in my hotels, the next time, we are going to kill you." I felt that I deserved it. Everything that I got, I deserved. In my heart I knew that I was guilty. They turned me over to the local police. I was glad because I thought my connection would fix everything up. As the police drove me away from the hotel, they began to ask me questions and punch me in the face. They called me all kinds of names. They blindfolded me and took me to the desert. Two police officers were involved. I said, "Why are you doing this to me?" One guy punched me and said, "Because you guys come to Las Vegas and you terrorize this city. You pull a bunch of robberies. Then we catch you. You pay the people off and we get stuck with all the paperwork. Then you leave. You make a lot of problems for us. We have families. We want to sleep and have peace at night. That's why!" He took a gun and cocked it. He said, "We are going to kill you." I said, "Go ahead. You are going to hell for killing me." He then drew his gun back and said, "Unless you promise us you will never come back again." I said, "Ok." They took me to the downtown police station and I called my attorney. My attorney called the Chief of Police. The Chief of Police and my attorney came to my cell. They apologized to me for the beating the officers gave me. They had no charges against me. They took me to the hospital. They mended me up and escorted me onto the plane, to leave Las Vegas.

When I went back East, it was 1972. While recovering from my bruises, the police violence and the violence of my life I still had no faith in God or in people. However, now that I was married, I felt that I needed to have a family. Some day I wanted to settle down and raise a family. Despite having no direction in life or a good education. But I remembered when I was a small boy in Italy. I was raised up to be optimistic. The word optimistic means to think positive. The strange thing is that, even though I had this belief in me, everything around me was the opposite. The environment in New York City, the people I associated with and the people surrounding my life were all humanistic. The word humanistic means someone who makes his own laws and disrespects the laws of the land. These people think about doing something and they do it with self justification.

I slowed down the adventure of jewel thieving and I got involved more in gambling, black-jack, horses, and poker. These were lesser crimes and there was less chance of going to jail. In spite of this, I had three misdemeanor charges pending and I was not free from the law yet. My lawyer continued to postpone the charges. The longer the better, until we got the right judge. The one who could be easily bribed. Hey, this was our way of life. Looking back now, I am ashamed of these things that I had done. I'm glad that I am writing this down. I am hoping that someone in a similar situation can stop and seek Godly wisdom or cry out to the Lord with true repentance and cease from all evil. The Bible says in 1 John 5:17: "All unrighteousness is sin." The word unrighteousness means to do wrong things or go the wrong way. There are people around the world, especially in New York City, who live like this. New York City is where immorality and violence and disorder runs wild. Unbelievably wild.

The idea of opening the restaurant failed and I took this as an opportunity to run card games. Every single night I ran games. Not only was I a notorious jewel thief, but now I am also a notorious gambler. In my way of running the club, people would come from all over New York City and New Jersey. Some would come with their girlfriends and get caught up in three days of gambling. The majority of them would lose their money and then ask for loans for their addictions, which were strong. They would lose control. Even the local police would gamble, lose their money and put their guns as collateral for a loan. During the week I had to go chase them down to get the loan money back. The majority of the clubs in New York City were controlled by the Mafia and the police were aware of it. When the police did not get their percentage they showed up without fear. They would break the games up, shut the place down and write a violation. I remember the connection I had with the Chief of Police and I took advantage of the protection. With each club I had to pay $4,000 dollars a month with the condition to stay low key and not make too much publicity. There were over thirty clubs in New York City running illegal card games.

Every one of them was getting shut down by the police. People were afraid to gamble there because they didn't want to get in trouble. When the owners of the clubs found out that I had protection from the police they all came to me for help. I expanded my protection to them and in return every club had to pay so much money to me. I would pay the police directly. It never failed that when we did not pay the police off they would come with batons and shut down the club. Even the police had their own way of running corruption in the city. Humanistically speaking, the police would make their own law. So who were the Mafia? The police were the Mafia too. This went on for a while. Because I was an optimistic, I began to take inventory and I did not like it. The more money I made, the more money I spent and the more money I lost. What comes to my mind is a scripture in the Bible:

Proverbs 5: 21-23
For the ways of man are before the eyes of the Lord, and he pondereth all his goings. His own iniquities shall take the wicked himself, and he shall be holden with the cords of his sins. He shall die without instruction; and in the greatness of his folly he shall go astray.

9
NEW LIFE IN CALIFORNIA DESTROYED BY DRUGS

As I began to feel more oppression and depression in my life, I wanted to escape. I realized that I had nowhere to go. I remembered that my brother Joe owned a pizza shop in New Jersey. I got the idea that I could go to California and start a new life and escape it all. However, in my mind I continued in the fast lane gambling. In the club I met this man named Pasquale who had an incredible underground connection in football. I joined in with him we began to beat the mafia book makers in Las Vegas. We were winning week after week and money was pouring in. My attorney informed me that my trial was approaching and that we could not postpone a court date. He said that because of my jewel thieving to expect three years in jail. My luck was running out and my freedom was running out. I had reached the end of the line. There were no more deals that could be made. Everything, to me, was becoming darker and darker.

Now that I look back I see it was the Lord all along trying to rescue me. It was like he was saying, "Bruno, stop all this activity of darkness. I have a better plan for you." There was the little voice inside of me. But I totally avoided it and continued with my desperation. I did things my way not God's way. The next Saturday and Sunday we bet more than twenty games on football. Believe it or not we lost 19 out of 20. After a good long talk with my wife Angela, we decided to move west. I made my plea of mercy to the courts. I told them that I wanted to have a new life out west and leave New York City and its nightlife. The courts accepted the plea with the condition of five years of formal probation. The District Attorney looked at my past record and saw that every five or six months I would get arrested. So they figured, let's give Bruno five years probation. They thought the law of averages was five or six months. They figured by giving me five years probation, that within five or six months I would break it, and then mandatorily I must do five years in prison. They were happy to negotiate this entrapment for me. But God was on my side and not only did I behave myself for five years but I went straight for more than twelve years.

As I continue with my journey you will see, step by step, the outcome. I released myself from any activity. I paid the bookmakers. I told the mafia that I'm quitting, that I had had enough. That God must have had another plan for my life. They all responded to me, "Carlo we love you, you're like one of us. You'll be back again." I said "No, no never. I am leaving for good." They began to plead with me to stay. To forget the money that I owed. They promoted me to 'Wiseguy', a boss. They said that I would never have to work a day in my life. That they would give me twenty five percent of New York. It was very tempting but I refused the offer. I abandoned it all and moved west.

Angela withdrew her savings, 25,000 dollars that she had saved, and we moved to Garden Grove, California. We opened a restaurant together with 15,000 dollars. Both of us began to work day and night. We began to make homemade bread and pizza. The place took off. The local police and the local baseball and soccer teams all began to brag that it was the best pizza in Orange County. Day after day I began to put my old life behind me. Now we were faced with a new challenge. I began to think about God and heaven. I remembered how I wanted to be a priest at five years of age back in Italy. My family, one by one, began to move to California to join me. Angela wanted to get pregnant and have a baby. We attempted to have a family but she had three miscarriages. The doctor found out Angela had a scarred tube on one side and a damaged ovary on the other side. This was due to an appendix surgery ten years before. Now that I look back I know that our sins were bringing a curse to our life. We were prisoners and victims of Satan. I did not believe it then but I believe it now. As a Catholic boy, they taught us that Satan was not real. But I know better now. All the bad things that I did were never meant to be. We did them because of lack of knowledge. The bible declares in Isaiah 4:6, "My people perish for lack of knowledge." Not only did we not have knowledge but we were not seeking God's laws. Somehow we had gone astray. I was working six days a week and on my day off I would love to go fishing to escape. To me fishing was heaven on earth.

As the years went by my niece and nephew moved to the area. I began to enjoy baseball and soccer and I got involved with the local youth soccer organization, A.Y.S.O. Not only did I coach but I was a referee. I began to feel good. I was thinking, "If I could do a lot of good works and dedicate my life to the community, someday I will go to heaven when I die." The business was prospering as we entered a new chapter in our lives. Meanwhile Angela was still trying to have a baby and she had five surgeries within three years. We purchased a home. She was a very sweet, hardworking lady and her dream was to give me a child. At this time none of us went to church and none of us knew how to pray. The doctors began to give Angela different kinds of medication. She took pills for ovaries, pills to wake- up, pills to go to sleep. She began to become addicted. One of the rules I had in my life, in the fast lane, was to never do hard drugs. I watched many acquaintances and friends and how their life was quickly destroyed by drugs. As my business began to grow my old life was never mentioned. I did not want people to know about my ugly past. I was very happy that I joined the local community. I belonged to a nice community and things were working out for the good. I even made some friends with the local police. Then disaster once again struck us. The local customers, for many years, requested that I would serve wine and beer. But I was afraid to apply for the license even though I only had a misdemeanor conviction and no felonies. Legally, I was informed that I would have no problem getting the license. I went to the local ABC and I applied for my liquor license. At the hearing I was rejected. The inspector had friends in Las Vegas. He made some phone calls and began to tell the local community about me. I got an attorney and we went to trial and I was granted the license. Then the inspector appealed it. The local police began to speak to me different and talk to me different. They took me for some kind of gangster.

While this was happening Angela began to smoke marijuana and she became addicted to snorting cocaine. This went on for three years.

From Mafia Boss to the Cross

This was all happening behind my back. It came to a point that I would make three thousand dollars a week. I would deposit the money and the checks would bounce the next day. I was naive and I was not being told. The local Mexican mafia would connect with her everyday. Behind my back they would make the appointment to drop off the drug. Me and my brothers would spend night after night gambling pinnacle amongst ourselves while Angela was running the business. The business began to drop and our bills grew bigger and bigger. I took a second mortgage on my store and my home. I even took a third mortgage in order to make it. I began to go to Gardena once a week to play poker. On Monday mornings I would go to Las Vegas to gamble and to place my football bets. This went on for several years. With Angela's addiction and my gambling addiction and without the support of the local police everything began to fall apart. It was 1980 when I came home from Las Vegas and found my wife on the floor with cut wrists. She had tried to commit suicide. I called 911 and they placed her into ICU. There she healed and after three months of 'psychological awareness' teaching, she was restored. I remember during the summer of 1982 that an undercover policeman came to my shop and claimed to be a businessman. As the weeks went by he began to ask me if I could put some bets in with the bookie. After he called in five or six bets, he came in with the police and identified himself as a policeman. They arrested me for accepting a bet. I was not a bookmaker. I was only a player and I was doing them a favor. We went to trial and the jury found me guilty of the conviction. The judge pled to the jurors. The judge asked, "Do you think Bruno should go to jail for this" the jury said "No." The judge said that the police were picking on me. That they should go after the big guy, not the small guy.

The bible declares that all gambling is idolatry and covetousness equals to witchcraft. (See Colossians 3:5) If you want to know more about this topic read my book "Honeymoon with the Holy Spirit." The judge knew better and he dismissed the case against me. This, however, costed me more money than I had. One month later the police who lost the case came to get even. One afternoon a Westminster undercover police claimed to be a construction co-worker. He told me he needed some money to buy food for his family and that in return he would give me a stereo. I accepted it and gave him fifty dollars and some food. Immediately his partners came in and arrested me for accepting illegal property. I should have known better, not to purchase anything from a person who has no license because this is a violation of the law. I didn't really care for the stinking stereo. I did this out of the goodness of my heart. In Garden Grove there are many poor people and families in need. Once again I was deceived. But now I am found by the master and I have learned to abstain from shady deals. But then, I found myself going to court and taking a plea. They gave me ninety days furlow. I would go in to county jail in the evening and come out in the morning to run my business. Shortly thereafter, Angela's addiction became worse. Dear reader, I hope you do not have anyone in your family that has gotten caught up like this. This addiction causes misbehavior and malfunctioning. You lose all values for life and cause destruction to people around you. Some people working with Angela in the restaurant were operating behind my back for their own gain. One afternoon I caught her stoned at home with more than two ounces of cocaine in her possession. We got into a big argument and I insisted she tell me who gave her the stuff. I wanted her to take it back and get the money. She wouldn't tell me. This went on for three years. I was fighting a losing battle. Without God's council and wisdom or help from the local church, I became desperate.

She would wreck cars and was gone for three or four days in a row. Finally she gave me names and addresses in Santa Ana. Furiously I called the police. I asked them to help me. Instead I got nothing but rejection. These officers who were once my friends, were now my enemies. Angela informed me that she gave these people four thousand dollars for the stuff that was poison. She told me that the people ripped her off. That evening I made up my mind that I was going to take the law into my own hands. I drove to Santa Ana. I went to the house of the connection that Angela gave me. I knocked on the door and this Mexican guy came to the door and said, "Bruno what are you doing here?" Not only did he sell drugs to my wife but now that I saw him, he was one of my best customers. He replied to me, "No, no, no, we don't sell anything to your wife. It's not me." I said, "You're lying" I reached for my thirty-eight and cocked it in his head. He kneeled down and began to cry. He said, "Please don't kill me. I'm not going to sell your wife drugs anymore." I said, "You people have destroyed our life. My wife is a mess and she's suicidal. She cut her wrists before." I said, "If you ever come back to my store and sell drugs to my wife I'm 'gonna come back here and kill you and your wife and kids." I said, "Now give me my money back and his wife opened the drawer and gave me 4,500 dollars."

Dear reader, even though he vowed he would not sell drugs to us anymore, these mafia people, they have no concept and no integrity. They have their friends and their cousins around to push the drugs. There is no honor. You see, I was fighting everybody on my own. I was trying to work with everyone to clean up the area. I saw my wife from 135 lbs. go down to 90lbs. The battle belongs to God. I didn't know then but I know now. I want to share with you that illegal drugs open up the mind and the body to demonic influence. Invasions of the supernatural demons to inflict your faculties and to destroy the very nature of God's creation. You see in Ephesians 6:10-18 it says: 'Put on the armor that ye may be able to stand against the fiery darts of spiritual wickedness in high places.' You see it is a spiritual warfare, only, I did not know then. After I got the money from the pusher, did Angela learn her lesson? No. Instead she got worse. I remember one Christmas day. I wanted it to be so beautiful. I went out to buy gifts for some families and then at 5p.m., the spirit of Christmas, was shut down in my marriage again. The first time, as I mentioned, my father died on

Christmas day. Now, disaster came in again. As I left Angela out of my sight for one hour I went to bring gifts to some of the children in the area. I came home one hour later and she was stoned, laid out on the floor. She began to argue and fight. She had fallen on the floor. I said, "Who are you, come out of her. I want my wife back." There was no change. Depression got a hold of me and frustration and desperation because for three long years I was fighting a lost battle. I opened her purse and I found a one ounce bag of cocaine. I was so depressed and frustrated that I shook her and I said, "Where did you get this?" I remember words came out of my mouth that were suicidal. For the first time in my life I wanted to die. I took the bag of cocaine and I shouted to Angela, "You're a junkie. You're going to die and I'm going to die with you. I swallowed all of the cocaine in the bag and overdosed immediately." Angela began to cry, "It's all my fault. I did this to you. I love you. I'll be a good wife, don't die." I felt that I was hallucinating.

That night I heard noises in my head. I heard people banging doors in my house, and I saw a man who had the shape of Satan. Finally, at

Dr. Bruno Caporrimo

9a.m., I slept several hours. I got up and went to work. I opened the restaurant that night at 10p.m. I was all alone and something inside of me arose. Something was building up inside of me. It felt like the enemy blinding me. I went home and drank a couple of Martinis. Angela was not there. I found out later that she went out to party with her friends. I could not sleep. I found myself all alone, frustrated, and I had an incredible desire to have some cocaine. I began to reject this feeling. I got in the car at 1:00 in the morning and drove to downtown Santa Ana. I found myself knocking on the door of the connection where, previously, I had the encounter. As he opened the door he was startled to see me. He shouted, "Bruno I have not been to your place anymore. Please leave me alone." I found myself saying to him, "Here's three hundred dollars. Get me some of the best cocaine!" He exclaimed to me, "No, no ,no, are you trying to set me up? I don't do this anymore!" I said to him, "If you know what is good for you get it now!"

I then realized that something had gotten a hold of me and my addiction kicked in. I always remembered the old days, people told me, "Once a junkie always a junkie." So now I knew that I was finished. Suddenly I realized that I was violating my own moral rules and regulations. The principal rule was to never give in to cocaine, hard drugs and illegal drugs. This was one of the reasons why I was still alive. Even though I was a notorious jewel thief and a gambler, among a few other things. Those were the dominant and controlling situations in my life. But I was not a junkie. Even the police knew me to be a clean and gentle jewel thief because I never condoned drugs. But I watched friends in high places and some in low places, since the early sixties, get involved in cocaine. They lost their very own life. They lost everything. Desperation, depression and the demon of drugs were knocking at my soul. You might say, "Brother Bruno, how do you know that this is the work of demons?" I did not know then but I know now because the bible declares in 1 Corinthians 9-11:

> Do you not know that the wicked will not inherit the kingdom of God? Do not be deceived; neither the sexually immoral nor idolators nor adulterers nor male prostitutes nor homosexual offenders nor thieves nor the greedy nor drunkard nor slanderers nor swindlers will inherit the kingdom of God. that is what

some of you were. But you were washed, sanctified, you were justified in the name of the Lord Jesus Christ and by the spirit of our God.

Wow, if I only knew then this passage I would have never done what I did. The real problem is that the Catholic church teaches that the devil is not real. They teach that Satan and his demons don't exist. I remember that, when I left New York City, I had taken a vow to myself that I would never steal or gamble ever again. That I would go to California to start a new life. The Bible declares that cursed is the man that trusts a man. For many years I kept myself pure because I wanted to do right with my life. Yet now I allowed the drugs to rule my life. I thought. "I will do this for a while. I'm strong enough to handle it and just use it as a pleasure." The truth of the matter is that it got worse and worse and worse. Now it is 2 p.m. on a Monday night, 1983, I am armed and dangerous with illegal drugs in my pocket. My heart was beating fast.

As I approached my home I saw that Angela's car was not in the driveway. A moment of happiness came to my mind. That I could be alone with my cocaine. That nobody would find out because I did not want nobody to know. At 3:00 in the morning I began to put the cocaine in my mouth. As I tasted the bitter and disgusting flavor, I swallowed a spoonful. My mouth, vocal chords, brain and body were all numb. A strange peace came up in me, like not being concerned or worried about anything. I felt no responsibility. I was not really enjoying myself. I felt lonely and strange. At 5:00 in the morning I began snorting through the nose more than a half ounce. I looked at my watch, it was 7 a.m. I tried to go to bed but I was wide awake. My body felt like a million pins and needles were pinching me. I began shaking and cried to God that I would never do this again. At 9 a.m. I managed to take a shower and dragged myself to open the restaurant. I worked until 4:00 in the afternoon. My employees relieved me. I went home and crashed and slept through the night. Two days later I confessed to Angela what I had done. We then agreed to get high together only from 9 to 12. We went and bought one ounce of pure cocaine. We began to celebrate together. Angela introduced me to a way to get high faster by inhaling the smoke of the cooked cocaine through a pipe. I experienced enjoyment and release with my bride. We got high and had a sexual romance. We went to work together thinking that we had everything under control. The next night we partied again. The addiction was costing us three-hundred dollars a day. I kept my word by doing this only in the night with my wife or a few other friends in secret. Several months went by and we began to lose control. Our lives weren't working at all and we began tumbling down. Angela was the total opposite of me. I tried to only party some nights but Angela's addiction got stronger. She was a solitaire type. She would disappear for three days in a row. Nowhere to be found. Our business demanded for us to be there on time and fully rested to bring supply and demand to the public. We began to show up late and we began to lose our regular customers. Bills began to pile up. In order to pay the bills we invited a couple of anonymous gambling friends in the local community. We opened up a social club in Garden Grove. Soon after we began to invite many people. We had card games seven nights a week. With the profit I managed to pay for my cocaine habit and some of the bills.

10
THE INVASION OF THE SWEET LOVE OF GOD

Sometime in 1983 Angela and I began a three day bash. We invited some cocaine friends and we had an all night splash. In the morning when everybody left Angela encouraged me to continue, both of us alone, to get high. We called the connection and he delivered the cocaine to our house. Believe it or not it was Saturday morning. The two of us snorted and smoked over two thousand dollars worth of cocaine. I admit that we couldn't stop. We were flowing in a strange ecstasy of self pleasure and we thought we had the world in our hands. We thought that we had everything under control. We were drinking Champagne, Rum, and inhaling cocaine. We had several employees who were running the business while we were hiding out from the world and reality. I remember very well that on Sunday night Angela pleaded with me, "Please let's go until 2 o'clock the next morning."

As we continued something very real and strange happened to us and to our home. Paranoia came in. Hallucination took over our very being and our souls. Suddenly fear and suspicion took over. It was so strong that we began to experience closets and doors being opened and slammed shut in the house. We panicked. I got a gun and we suspected there was someone inside the house. The noise was so violent. Every room we went into, we heard the doors slam shut and footsteps. People were running up and down in the attic and basement

Dr. Bruno Caporrimo

and outside in the backyard. We were so afraid. It was supernatural. There was some demonic power in my home. I know now that we were demon possessed. I didn't believe it then. What was going through my mind was that maybe it was a drug dealer or a gang doing this to us. We went from the bedroom to the den and the back door at, 3:00 in the morning, slammed shut. It was like images of men, spiritually, were running away from the house. Noise began to come down from the attic. A thundering noise. It felt like there were about ten people there. Angela and I finally ran out of the front door and rushed to our next door neighbor. At 3:00 in the morning we called 911. Over a dozen police arrived. The local police knew me. I said to them that there were thieves in my home. They surrounded the house and went in with a full inspection. They came out declaring to us that whoever it was left the house. Dear reader, at 3:30 we went back inside the house and we slept more than ten hours. We vowed that we would quit and get cleaned up.

Several days later we joined a health spa and a group in Newport Beach called 'Awareness.' It was a group of doctors who taught meditation and that you could overcome any addiction. Three months went by and Angela and I gained our weight back. We began lifting weights and went to our 'Awareness' classes. We were doing pretty well, however, we were still tempted from time to time. But we were straight for three months. Both of us began to focus, to rebuild our restaurant and gain our reputation back with our local customers. I was spending some of my free time playing poker in a local club. I was hoping that I could win some money to catch up with the bills. Instead I was getting deeper and deeper in financial bondage.

A short time later tragedy struck again. On a Friday afternoon at 2:30 in 1984, I gave Angela 1,500 dollars to go to Smart and Final and purchase some wholesale groceries. She gave me a smile and a kiss and she said, "I'll be back in a little while." Friday nights were big nights. I'm sure you understand that having a deli, pizza shop and a bakery with delivery service, would take full faculties of the mind and a lot of devotion to the work to be successful. We were focusing and meant well but the enemy of our soul, the spirit of addiction, was knocking again. It was attacking the weaker vessel! Thirty minutes went by when two local police stood and knocked on my front door. They said, "Are you Bruno?" I replied, "Yes." The police responded, "You need to come with us. Your wife is in trauma. She got ran over by a car." I responded, "No!! Where?" He said, "Around the corner at the 7-11." I immediately ran there. It was about one block from the restaurant. I saw that twenty people lifted up the car and pulled Angela from under the car. As I arrived the ambulance were taking off. I broke down. I was crying and screaming. The police were holding me back and trying to calm me down. The paramedics rushed her to Fountain Valley Hospital. She was placed in Emergency. I had never had any prayer in my life. I had always tried to do things with my own strength. I waited in the waiting room. The doctor informed that her pelvis was broken and 80% of her liver was cut off. Her pelvic and tale bone and 70% of the flesh from her rear were ripped apart. The doctor advised me to sign for surgery stating that she only had a 30% chance of living.

I found out later that Angela, instead of going to Smart and Final, went to the liquor store to call her connection with the money. While she was waiting for her connection, someone tried to steal the car. It was a 1972 Oldsmobile and the idle needed an adjustment. It would take off fast. Angela got behind the car and tried to hold the car from rolling back. Her sandals got stuck and the car went through her and cut the lungs and all her chest. The man in the gas station rushed to her aid with the car-jack and jacked up the car. But because he rushed, the car fell on top of Angela. He tried a second time and the jack fell again. Dear reader, talk about pain, agony and punishment. When I found this out I was brokenhearted, hoping that she would be okay. All my family and friends rushed to the hospital. My brother Sal, my sister-in-law and my brother Bob were all born again Christians and they knew how to pray. After seven hours of surgery, Angela was put in Intensive Care. She remained in a coma while there were several people praying for us. I buried myself in my work and visited the hospital. Seven days went by and I remembered there was no change with Angela. The following week I was told that the hospital bill would be more than $100,000. I had no medical insurance. I was planning a way to get the money because I wanted to pay the hospital. I scraped about $15,000 dollars together and I was thinking, on the weekend, to go to Las Vegas. In my mind I was thinking that this time I was going to win.

In the middle of that week God sent a sweet, gentle man to me. His name was Roy Lang. I shared the tragedy of the accident and what was going on in my life. He wanted to go to the hospital and pray for Angela. I accepted his offer because there was something special about this man. He was gentle, kind and compassionate. The next several days we went to the hospital together. Roy was carrying a big bible and while he was driving he would plant seeds into my mind. He would share the gospel with me and I was feeling really good listening to him. In the past, many, many customers tried to witness to me about the Lord. I would always respond by showing them my crucifix saying, "Jesus is right here. See, I got him hanging on the wall." "I also have a very large tapestry of Jesus, and on my neck I got him." The truth of the matter is that I was a fool and blind to the things of God. All I had was head knowledge of religion. But not relationship. Even though this man had some thing special I was still set in my own traditional ways. I wished that I had his character and personality. That Friday afternoon I mentioned to Roy that I would go to Vegas and that I needed to make some money. His response was, "Don't go, gambling is wrong. You will not prosper. You need to stop and you need to ask the Lord to forgive you of your sins." I responded to him rudely and vulgarly. I said, "I don't have any sins and I'm not a sinner. So shut-up and don't talk to me like that anymore. I know what I'm doing and there's nothing wrong with playing poker." I remember now that I was very rude. He did not deserve that. But I remember him saying to me that I was a sinner. I could not accept that. Please do not put this book down. The best is yet to come, as the pages unfold to you. The Bible says in 1 John 1: 8-9,

> If we claim to be without sin, we deceive ourselves and the truth is not in us. If we confess our sins, he is faithful and just and will forgive us our sins and purify us from all unrighteousness. If we claim we have not sin, we make him out to be a liar and his word has no place in our lives.

That Friday night I escaped. I left everything behind me one more time. I was thinking that once again, I would make it big in Vegas. I had $15,000 in my pocket. I went to the Stardust casino and I played blackjack from 9 to 12. I won $45,000. Now, with $60,000 in my pocket the casino manager, who knew me, gave me a free comp. I could have anything I wanted to eat, anything I wanted to drink, and

From Mafia Boss to the Cross

the best room in the hotel because I was a high roller. I went to sleep and at 9:00 in the morning I began to play poker, until 3:00 Sunday morning. Angela was still in a coma. I remember that Roy put a pager on the bed with a voice mail and twice a day I would call Angela. That Sunday afternoon some old friends came around and introduced me to a lady. She was beautiful. Her father owned one of the casinos. She told me that two basketball games were fixed and would be a guaranteed win. Well, I bet all of the $60,000. I went to the window and bet those games and we went out and celebrated with Rose. She took me to her apartment and there I committed adultery again. At that time I did not believe that it was adultery. I was like a blind mule. I believed that if nobody caught you that you could get away with it. Then you were safe. The truth of the matter is, we have a spy in the sky and that is God our Father. He forbids sin and he loves his children. He hates for them to do wrong.

I was swallowed up by her looks and her charm. We got drunk and I began telling her all my problems. I was hoping that I could release my pain. It was now 11:30 on a Sunday night. I went to the booking window to look up the results of the games and check the scoreboard. I lost both games by a half point. I lost all the money. I felt guilty, ashamed and broke. Suddenly I began thinking about the words that a Christian brother, Roy taught me. I am a sinner. His words were ringing in my ear like a bullet aiming to my heart. I took a late flight home. I arrived on Monday morning. As I entered my house I took an inventory of my life. I began to scream like never before, aloud. I blamed God for everything that was happening to me. I pulled down the crucifix and began to punch, many times, the rug of the twelve apostles and Christ eating the last supper. I said out loud, over and over and over, "God it's your fault. Where are you? Why do you let me suffer like that? Who am I? Help me, I don't want this life anymore." I broke down and began to cry. For the first time in my life I'm crying.

Dear reader, I remind you that I was beat up by the police in New Jersey, New York City, Las Vegas, Puerto Rico and many times stabbed or shot at, but I never cried. I was always an optimistic hypocrite, looking for a way out. Now I am crying unto the Lord. Really crying. I fell down on my knees, broken, with no strength left in me. I was broken and squashed down. I remember the words of the Evangelist. They came to me very loud saying, "I am a sinner. I need Jesus in my life." These very words, suddenly, were real and sweet and easy to proclaim because they came alive in my mind. For the first time in my life I was being shot by a spiritual bullet from God and all his power of conviction was coming down invading the house, the room, and my soul. I opened my mouth and proclaimed, "Yes God, I am a sinner. Lord Jesus come to my life. Take over Lord, I need you." Suddenly the room's atmosphere changed. A sweet breeze took over my heart, mind and soul and filled me with the anointing of the Holy Spirit. Supernaturally my soul was being freed from all demonic influence. All the shame, guilt, fear and condemnation that I had been carrying for forty-five years was being removed by the power of the Master. I fainted, flat on my face. I was as weak as a dead man for a few minutes. I knew that I was born again. BORN AGAIN FROM ABOVE WHICH THE BIBLE CONFIRMS IN 2 CORINTHIANS 5:17,

> So therefore anyone who is in Christ he is a new creation. All things are past away and behold all things have become new. Now everything is from God, Who Reconciled us to Himself through Christ and gave us the Ministry of Reconciliation!!

I felt the invasion of the sweet love of God! The sweet anointing embraced me and his manifestation took over my mind with a new revelation. I was before the King of kings and Lord of lords. I saw the Lord standing, in the spirit, face to face with me.

You might want to say, "How can this be possible." Well, the bible declares in John 14:21,

> Whosoever has my commandments and obeys them, he is the one who loves me. He who loves me will be loved by my father and I too will love him and show myself to him.

WOW!! With my broken heart before the Lord, his supernatural manifestation began to unfold the healing power through me. It was like healing fire burning the drinking, drugs, and the substances that were pinning me down. He took 45 years of pain out of my life. I cried out to the Lord to heal Angela too. I said, "Lord heal Angela. If you do

From Mafia Boss to the Cross

that I will serve you forever, do anything for you and go anywhere. In my mind I saw the impression and the image and the expression of the Lord open up his mouth and lift his hand to heaven and say, "Ask my Father in my name and I will do it." (See John14:14) His love and his power came into my life. This was all something new to me. It was so beautiful. It was beyond what words can express about the love of God. I remember getting up and walking away full of the love of God and I was saying to myself, "He is real, he is real, he loves me." I marveled at this experience and encounter. I heard many Christians talk about experiences like this, but it was hard to accept it. Now it happened to me.

You read in the bible about how God appeared to Abraham, a regular man who came from idol worshipping. A very common man and God changed and transformed him. Now, it is my turn. Many people need this experience. My turning point was when I kneeled down at the end of my wits, at my point of crossroads, he heard my cry and rescued me from the grasp of Satan. This is the true God of Abraham, Issac and Jacob that is only found in Christ Jesus. There is no other way. He IS the only way. Now that he found me, I will never let go. It don't matter what it takes. If everybody forsakes me or if I lose everything that I got, I will never forsake him. My new life and experience with God and evil began to be very real. Three or four hours had 'gone by and I was on cloud nine. A short time later I drove to my restaurant. Several minutes later my brother Joe came running towards me. He was screaming, "Where have you been for three days? You no good bum! Angela died one hour ago!" I said, "No Joe, it's not true. I am a Christian now." He responded, "You're a liar and a thief and a gangster!" He threw the car keys at my face. I grabbed his arm. I said, "No Joe, stop. Listen to me. He turned around and punched my nose. While I was bleeding I went to fight back like I always did before. I went to punch him and curse at him. An angel grabbed my tongue and arm and I was hopeless to move. Even one of my employees said, "Bruno, fight back." I began to cry again. I went home because I needed to find God again. I needed for him to give me his strength again. I kneeled down while tears ran down my cheeks. The Holy Spirit invaded my life again. I said to the Lord, "I hate my brother Joe. He doesn't believe me. Lord, it will be you and me all the way." Then suddenly, I turned around and the Bible fell to the floor from the desk. Roy had given it to me. I was startled from the noise, I turned around, and the word from 1 John came to my attention. It says in 1 John 15:

> Whosoever hateth his brother is a murderer and yea know that no murderer hath eternal life abiding in him.

This scripture penetrated my heart like a spiritual bullet. Now God is dealing with me one on one. I was not dealing any longer with gangsters or the police. Now it was direct. God and me. And God means business! Believe me, God was getting my attention because His love and correction were not humanistic. They were Heavenly sweet. I wanted all that God had for me. I was a prisoner of sin for forty-five years. A prisoner of darkness who was now found. I wanted to be connected to God. At this point you might say, "Bruno, are you sure that God dropped the Bible on the floor?" Well, why not? Did God not knock down Paul the Apostle from his horse? He was a murderer and a thief and God struck him down. The Lord struck down Paul on the way to Damascus (See Acts 9:1-2). How much more would God do for a little ex-jewel thief like me. At the time, when the Lord knocked the Bible down from the table, I did not know anything about the Holy Spirit or the Holy Angels. But I did not question. I just believed it. Simple faith can move mountains. After reading the scripture I quickly kneeled down and I said, "Lord forgive me, save him too." I stood bare on my knees for quite a while enjoying his presence. Sometime later Roy, the 'evangelist like angel', came to my house. He took me to the hospital. The doctors and nurses had taken off all her tubes. She had already been dead a couple hours. In my heart I never accepted it, even though she was dead. God's visitation had already filled me with his faith. I asked the nurse if I could go inside the room. She said, "Yes." There was Angela covered up with a sheet. Roy opened up the Bible and I said to the nurse, "We're going to pray." She shouted to me, "Are you crazy? She's already dead." I shouted, "Please leave the room, leave us alone." I kneeled down crying and praying and the power of God fell. All the gifts of the Holy Spirit were in operation. I watched God at work! It was just like when he opened up the Red Sea in the Ten Commandments. When Charles Heston pointed the rod and

From Mafia Boss to the Cross

the Red Sea opened up. Now this was happening to me and it is not a movie. It's real, simple faith. The room was full of this power and God supernaturally gave me spiritual eyes to experience his love and power at work. Supernaturally he was pushing all the sickness and pain caused by the accident. Pushing out the demons and the angel of death that had entered Angela's body. In a matter of seconds Angela opened her eyes. She began to cry. She was happy and she was kissing me. She experienced salvation right then and there. She was BORN AGAIN. The Lord made a miracle. The power of the Holy Spirit was like an explosion. It touched many people in that hospital. There was a change of direction for me and Angela.

In my joy I called the nurses as they walked in, they were overwhelmed seeing Angela alive and they shouted, "Hallelujah." Within minutes the news was all over that big hospital. They removed her from the ICU into a regular room. Three days later Angela was sent home. Everyone in the hospital celebrated the supernatural miracle. The real miracle was the new birth. Both of us knew the transformation now because neither one of us desired drugs or liquor anymore. Angela was released from the hospital in a wheelchair because her rear-end was totally ripped off. God gave me so much love for her. I began everyday to lay hands on Angela and pray over her. I began experiencing everyday this new life which was the power of the Holy Spirit. Within three months, because we had a daily prayer life, Angela was totally healed. I knew then that God empowers people with 'Healing Ministry.' In spite of the trials we were going through with bill collectors, we trusted God. I knew in my heart that God had called me and that I was to serve him. But I did not know exactly what to do. Thank God for brother Roy. For three months he took us to a very special church called, 'Eagle's Nest' in Santa Ana, California. The pastor was a very well known and respected World Evangelist named Gary Greenwald. I attended his church for several months and I began taking a foundation course in Biblical Theology. I attended every meeting and I would go to the fellowship meetings at every opportunity I had. It was a very balanced church. There was great worship and good preaching of the Word. In one meeting that I attended the pastor called me out and began to pray for me.

He gave me a prophecy. He said, "Bruno, the Lord is saying to you that you will be an Evangelist, a Prophet and an Apostle. God is raising you up and will train and equip you to send you to the nations." I felt the fire of the Holy Spirit come upon me and immediately I was filled with an incredible joy. I must admit to you that it has been twenty-one years and God has been faithful in many ways. In many ways and in many blessings which I will be sharing with you as the pages unfold in this journey.

While Angela was recovering I took on the work in the restaurant. I knew that I was not the same person anymore. I knew that we must now follow the plan and purpose of God for our lives. To fulfill the destiny of his purpose through many trials and tribulations. I decided to follow him, no matter what, so that I could fulfill my dream of what was ahead. Of my journey. I decided to focus, no matter what life threw at me. I would continue to be faithful. That was my prayer to the Lord. The Bible declares, 'To whom much is forgiven, much is required." The Apostle Paul declares,

"I was chief among sinners." God by his grace had forgiven me and called me in the ministry because what I did, I did in ignorance. I was ignorant of his law. The Lord began to bring all new people around me. He brought to me real estate people and restaurant owners who were interested in buying my restaurant. A wonderful dream began to unfold. Within several months I had my home, the restaurant property, everything sold.

Day after day I was talking about the Lord to my family, friends and customers. Many of them rejected my preaching. Many would say to me, " Bruno, I have no time to listen to you. I want a sandwich. I have to go back to work." Others would shake their heads, startled, and could not understand what had happened to me. Regardless of the negativity towards my Christianity, I would not give up because I wanted to share with the whole world about my experience with God. In spite of everyone that rejected me, I continued for many years to preach the Gospel. New relationships with those who disagree with us certainly should not start with criticism, admonishment, scolding, rebuke, or argument. Such negative communication threatens authentic communication. It causes emotions to be on the defensive, embarrassed, or angered. After twenty years in the ministry I have learned a fundamental principle that I have used in my communications. To always begin conversation with someone who seems to be an adversary by trying first to focus on what you can agree on. For example; a common danger and your need for each other or ways of helping each other. Perhaps both of you share a positive value like, classical music or sports. Or it may be moral values that you have in common. After discovering what you agree on, you are on the path to building a respectful relationship. Communication at its best is always artfully spoken and carefully seeks to seize upon areas where agreement is possible. Where hopes and hurts can be shared. As well as dreams, discouragements, faith and fears. This is the emotional soil where powerful communication can happen.

I was not taught this 'art' of communication when I studied to be a preacher. I was trained to preach sermons. In my first year of practice I failed to win an audience. "Stop preaching and start witnessing," was a lesson I had to learn for myself. I discovered purely by accident that people don't want to be preached to. They want to be helped and encouraged honestly and sincerely. That is the secret of effective communication. Start by being sensitive to the hurting and troubled heart. Share how positive faith inspires, encourages and lifts the spirit. I challenge and motivate my listeners to discover and embrace positive thinking. Every person needs that. That's the classic path to success. Find a need and fill it. Find a hurt and heal it. Find a problem and solve it. When you find a disagreement, bridge it. "You shall be called a repairer of the breach and a restorer of paths to dwell" (Isaiah 58:12). This has been my lifelong guideline in communication. My goal is not to make people feel guilty and fearful of punishment. Instead, I now target the hurts in their hearts.

11
HEAVEN OPENED AND THE FIRE CAME DOWN

I continued to go to church at 'Eagles Nest' and I had a great desire concerning the things of the Lord. A desire to learn all that I could about the Lord and about the Holy Spirit. I attended many different Christian meetings in the area. Day after day, while running my business, I continued to witness to my customers. Many would say to me, "Bruno stop preaching to me. I go to church every Sunday!" Oh, how I wanted people to know about my new Honeymoon with the Holy Spirit. During this time in my walk with the Lord, I began to know for certain that I wanted to serve the Lord full time, and tell people about Jesus. Tell people about his love, his power and all my experiences with him. People kept on rejecting me. I knew that I needed to be trained and discipled. And that I needed to go to Bible College.

Several days later I was told there was going to be a big revival in Anaheim. I was told about a ministry called 'Melodyland.' The pastor of this church was named Ralph Wilkerson. I was told that they had men's prayer meetings every Thursday morning at 6:00 a.m. One Thursday I went. I met about 30 men of God who truly knew how to pray. I also met a Pastor named Nielson who was standing in the office of a prophet. He was also a teacher and he taught us many truths of God's Word and the Holy Spirit. I became his disciple. In every meeting that I attended, during prayer, I would see Jesus when looking at that man.

From Mafia Boss to the Cross

After several months I was clearly growing in the knowledge of the Lord and experiencing his mighty power in so many manifestations of the Spirit. But I still had not been baptized in water. I thought about this and soon after, I requested to be baptized in the swimming pool. I wanted an experience of baptism like Jesus had with John the Baptist. I really desired this with all my heart. The Lord met me fully in my desire.

One Sunday afternoon a group from my church gathered for my baptism. They began singing the song, "I have decided to follow Jesus." I entered the water with my Pastor and he dunked me under the water three times. He did this to Angela also. I was baptized in the name of God the Father, God the Son, and God the Holy Spirit in Jesus' name. As I came up out of the water for the third time I swam to the edge of the pool and sat on the cement ledge. I felt so fresh, new, clean and alive. While looking up at the sky I began to pray in the Spirit. I then saw heaven open. The sky disappeared and my whole being was filled with the Holy Spirit. It was flooding through me like a great water torrent. I raised my hands to heaven and said, "Father, father, Abba, father. I want more and more from You. Don't let this experience disappear!" I continued to see the glory of God coming in and all around me like liquid fire from above. Now I could truly say that I had experienced being baptized with the Holy Spirit and fire. I sincerely hope this experience can be repeated in the lives of every one of you, dear readers. The bible declares in Matthew 3:16:

> And Jesus, when he was baptized, went up straight way out of the water; and, lo, the heavens were opened unto him, and lighting upon him.

That evening I was still praying in the Spirit and singing to the Lord when I heard a knock on the door. As I opened it some of my old friends came to see me. When they saw me so happy they began to marvel. I invited them to sit. I picked up the bible to read to them. They began shaking there heads saying, "Bruno has gone crazy, let's go." They left and I never saw them again. I realized that they expected something else of me, like the old man of the past. As I sat there, in the prescence of the Lord, I began to pray for them. I said to the Lord, "What is going on? Why am I so strange to them? I opened up the bible and this is what I read;

Ephesians 2:2
Wherein in time past ye walked according to the course of this world, according to the prince of the power of the air, the Spirit that now worketh in the children of disobedience.

2 Corinthians 4:4
In whom the God of this world hath blinded the minds of them, which believe not, lest the light of the glorious gospel of Christ, who is the image of God, should shine unto them.

I concluded that they were making fun of me because once I too, in the past, would make fun of people like me who were born again Christians.

EXPERIENCING THE SUPERNATURAL – FACE TO FACE WITH SATAN

During the night I was awakened from my deep sleep by a noise coming from the backyard patio. As I opened my eyes, the living room lights suddenly went on. I got up to turn the lights off and then all of a sudden the lights went off. I was so drowsy that I thought I was dreaming. I was so tired I fell asleep again. A short time later I felt hands grab my tee shirt and drag me to the end of the ten-foot couch. I was startled and choking. When I opened my eyes I saw Satan right in front of my face. He began to growl at me. Instantly, I felt fear and could smell a bad odor in the room. With a choking breath I managed to shout at the devil, "The blood of Jesus." Immediately I was free. I jumped to my feet with my hands clenched and my arms defiantly up in the air. I shouted again, "Jesus, Jesus!" Suddenly there was peace in the room. I immediately got down on my knees and began to pray, calling on the Lord saying, "Lord, I need you. Why is this happening to me? Help me!" I suddenly remembered all the times in church I had heard that the power was in the blood of Jesus! I began praying again, saying, " Lord Jesus, I come to the cross of Calvary. Cover me with Your blood."

In the peace that came I was suddenly caught up in the Spirit again. While in the spirit, a vision came to me. I saw the cross of Calvary. There were a man and a woman taking Jesus down from the cross and carrying him to the tomb. Then my vision ended. I was on my knees again praying by the couch. I fell asleep right there on my knees. In the morning, as the sun came through the windows, I awoke. I was still feeling disturbed by what had happened that night. I got up and called Pastor Nielson. Remember, he was a prophet. I shared with him everything that had happened that previous night. He said to me, "Bruno, God has a tremendous calling on your life and Satan is trying to stop you. Once you served him and now he's lost you. He is angry with you. He came to you last night to try to frighten you back to him. The Lord is preparing you to take you into the wilderness to fast and pray and to give you his vision for your life and ministry. I warn you to stay close to the Lord and put on the whole armor of God." (Ephesians 6:10-17: Finally my brethren, be glad in the Lord and put on the whole armor of God to stand the evil one.) I said, "Thank you Pastor Nielson. I am blessed by your words. Thank you!" Before miracles He was led to temptation. Many people were surprised to read that after the Lord Jesus was mightily filled with the Holy Spirit, that he was immediately led by the Holy Spirit into the greatest temptation of his life. In Mark 1:12 it says, "The Holy Spirit drove him into the wilderness." In Matthew 4:1-4 it says,

> Then was Jesus led by the spirit into the wilderness to be tempted of the devil. And when he had fasted 40 days and 40 nights, he was afterward hungered. And when the tempter came to him, he said, "If thou be the son of God, command that these stones be made bread." But he answered and said, "It is written, man shall not live by bread alone, but by every word that proceedeth out of the mouth of God."

It was only after the Lord's anointing by the Holy Spirit that he had his encounter with Satan face to face. This was his life's greatest temptation. Through the Holy Spirit Jesus was made strong enough to take the offensive against temptation. Instead of avoiding them. You see, Christ came to break the power of sin. Instead of waiting for Satan to come at his time, the Holy Spirit led Christ right away to a face to face confrontation with him so that Satan's power could be broken by the God-man. Before Christ began his ministry, nine important things happened:

1. He was baptized.
2. He was anointed and empowered by the Holy Spirit.
3. He was led into the wilderness by the Holy Spirit to confront Satan and break his power.
4. He came down from the mountain and preached the gospel saying, "Repent, the kingdom of God is at hand."
5. He healed the broken hearted.
6. He taught, preached and did deliverance.
7. He brought sight to the blind, and to those in darkness, he gave them light.
8. He brought freedom to those who were bruised by satan and in need of emotional healing.
9. He proclaimed salvation for all humanity.

These nine points are crystal clear! The Savior did all these things after the Holy Spirit empowered Him and filled Him with the love of the Father. He demonstrated His honeymoon for the bride. If the Savior did all this, and then died for us to give us his life and victory in all things, how much more are we able to do through Him? How can we ever forget this? Anointed and endued with the power of the Holy Spirit, I continued my journey with the Lord at 'Melodyland'. I attended Pastor Nielson's healing services. One evening he was teaching on the subject of anointing oil. On the meaning and purpose of oil in scripture. He advised each of us to carry a bottle of oil for anointing the sick. From that day forward I carried a bottle of oil in my pocket everywhere I went. Each day I began to anoint myself with the oil. I also anointed the people with whom I worked in the ministry. The Bible declares in 1 Samuel 16:1, "And the Lord said to Samuel, how long will thou mourn for Saul, being I have rejected him from reigning over Israel. Fill thine horn with oil, and go, I will send thee to Jesse the Bethlehemite;

for I have provided me a king among his sons." Then we see in verse 12 that Samuel took the horn of oil and anointed him in the midst of his brethren. The Spirit of the Lord came upon David from that day forward. It is crystal clear through this passage that David as a young shepherd boy of 13, although he was an Israelite, had at this time no concept of the works of the Holy Spirit. I am sure he had knowledge of the scriptures of his fathers; Abraham, Noah, Isaac, Joseph and all the prophets up to that time. But he was not yet anointed and endowed with the power of the Holy Spirit. We can see how God raised up Samuel to anoint David as a king. The anointing came upon David through the oil from the horn. The Holy Spirit then rested upon David from that moment on and the honeymoon began. The Holy Spirit carried David through trials, tribulations, wars, agonies, oppression, depression, weeping, crying, lamenting, mourning and failure into victories. His example is for all humanity. His songs, psalms and writings are a pattern of his life. We must understand that he could not have accomplished all these things in his life without the power of the Holy Spirit working in him.

THE PERSONALITY OF THE HOLY SPIRIT

It is of great importance that we believe in the divinity and power of the Holy Spirit and also His personality. It is only when we learn these truths that we can give Him the honor, worship, adoration and personal respect that we give to God. We must learn that the Holy Spirit is not a mere power that we need to get hold of and use. We must learn that He is God who is infinitely wise, holy, just and gracious, and who seeks to get hold of us and use us. We must become acquainted with Him not merely as an influence or power. The following points from Scripture prove that:

* Pronouns are used of Him (John 14:16-26; 15:26; 16:7-15).
* Personal attributes are ascribed to Him (Hebrews 9:14; Luke 1:35; 1 Corinthians 2:10-11; John 14:16-17; 15:26; 16:13-15; Acts 2:4).
* Personal works are ascribed to Him (Psalms 104:30; Romans 9:11; Matthew 12:28; John 16:7-11).
* Personal treatment is ascribed to Him (Acts 7:51; 5:9; Ephesians 4:30; Matthew 12:31-32; Hebrews 6:4-6; Philippians 2:1).

In the Holy Spirit is relationship for men. He is spoken of as searching hearts, regenerating, sanctifying, helping, convicting, teaching, guiding, witnessing, interceding, revealing, working, hearing, speaking, helping, communing, appointing, commanding, counseling, comforting, inspiring, assuring, calling, and in many ways, acting as a real person. A person is anyone who can think, feel and act. Anyone capable of self-consciousness and self-determination. Any individual having legal rights and duties; a rational being with bodily presence, soul passions, and spirit faculties. If this is true of the Holy Spirit, as we have seen in all the facts mentioned above, then there is nothing in Scripture that is clearer. How could the Holy Spirit do all the things spoken of as God, and have many divine personal names, titles, offices, acts, attributes, and receive personal pronouns? We must conclude that the Holy Spirit is the Spirit of Christ if we want to harmonize all Scripture. (If you want to know more about who the Holy Spirit is, please read our book, "Honeymoon with the Holy Spirit".)

FULL GOSPEL BUSINESS EXPERIENCE WITH HEALING

One day I was invited to a meeting of the Full Gospel Business Men's Fellowship International in Santa Ana, California. One of the leaders, Ron Weinbender, said there was a lady in a hospital nearby. He asked me to go and pray for her healing. She had a bad back condition. I said I would love to go. That it would be a privilege for me to go and pray for her. He gave me the directions to the hospital and the room number. I was so excited to be going on a mission for the Lord. I took my Bible and oil, and I was out the door. When I arrived at the hospital, I quickly went to the first floor, room 135. This was the room number Ron had given me. I entered the room very quietly. I was somewhat uneasy because I had no official papers stating that I could be in this public place to pray for a sick person. In the room everything was quiet. An elderly lady in bed, looked up and greeted me. I could see she was in pain. She saw my Bible and asked if I had come to pray for her. I said, "Yes." I took my Bible and read to her from James 5:13-14. Then I took my oil and anointed her and spoke to the demon of pain and agony in her back. Suddenly she jumped up from the bed and shouted, "Hallelujah! Praise the Lord." Her shouting caused the nurse to come into the room. The nurse told her to lie down because she was not feeling well. The nurse tried to put her back into bed. The woman said, "Get away from me. Jesus healed me, I am going home." She started to get dressed. The nurse then turned to me and pointed her finger at me with an angry face and said, "Are you responsible for this? At that, I left the room quickly. I practically ran out of the hospital and went home.

WRONG ROOM

That evening the phone rang and it was Ron Weinbender. He said, "Bruno, you have let me down. How can you expect to be a good minister for God if you don't do what you say you will do?" I said, "What do you mean? What are you talking about?" He said, "I am talking about you not going to the hospital today as you said you would." I said, "Ron, I was there where you told me to go, to room 135." He said to me, "What room did you go to?" I responded, "Building B." He said, "That is building B. She is in building A. You went to the wrong building." I said, "But Ron, I prayed for that lady even though it was the wrong building, and she got healed. She heard God's Word, believed, and was healed. That's fantastic." This was such an amazing experience in God's truth and the power of His Word. A lady was healed by hearing and believing God's Word. In spite of being the wrong assignment It was a blessing. This lady was not in any way waiting or expecting anyone to come to her. She simply heard the Word, believed, and received the miracle. Can you imagine if the body of Christ around the world would rise up and visit hospitals in every area where they live? I am sure we could empty the hospitals. Not to mention the multitudes that would be saved and be assured of an eternity in heaven, and would experience forever an awesome honeymoon with the Holy Spirit in Christ Jesus.

REVIVAL WITH R.W. SCHAMBACH

Early in 1986, I continued my fellowship at 'Melodyland' and the bible studies with Pastor Nielson. My house and business were still up for sale. At this time, I continued to see how the Lord was working in my life and moving me from glory to glory. At this time, 'Melodyland' was having a three day spiritual revival meeting with Pastor R. W. Shambach, the well known healing and revival Evangelist. The church requested volunteers to be ushers for this event. I fasted and prayed before it started, and the next day I went to report for duty as an usher. There was a long line of people at the door already, waiting for the service to start. I entered the building to receive my usher's badge and instructions. I heard a great commotion in the parking lot a few yards from where I was entering. I ran to the parking lot and there was a crowd of people looking down at a middle-aged black lady, very heavy set, lying on the pavement. People were shouting, "She had a heart attack! She's dead! Call the police. Call an ambulance."

My first reaction was to pull the bottle of oil out of my pocket as I ran and knelt beside the dead woman. I anointed her with oil on her forehead and commanded the angel of death to leave her. I prayed for the Holy Spirit to bring life to her. I then continued to pray according to James 5:14, which says, "Is any sick among you? Let him call for the elders of the church and let them pray over him, anointing him with oil in the name of the Lord." Suddenly her eyes shot open. She looked straight at me with a smile on her face and said, "Oh, thank you." At this time I heard people shouting, "Here come the police and the ambulance!" The police began separating the people to get to the patient. Medics from the ambulance began to connect a heart detector to her. I had moved away from the crowd and was praying, "Dear Lord, thank you for healing this lady. I know satan is trying to ruin this healing and revival service tonight but I thank you because you have intervened once again."

As I went closer to where the lady was being treated by the paramedics, I heard one of them say to her, "Looking at your records on the computer, you have a history of heart attacks and high blood pressure. But I don't find the heart scars that are recorded. Your heart is in perfect condition and your blood pressure is normal. What happened to you?" The woman said she collapsed and felt she was dying. Then she heard a man praying for her and when she opened her eyes, she saw me leaning over her and praising the Lord. After hearing that, I slipped away and went inside filled with just joy. I continued to praise the Lord. What Satan meant for wrong, God meant for good! (See Romans 8:28) The 'Spiritual Revival' meeting was a total success for the Lord. For three days, many people got healed, delivered from oppression, and saved. From my experience in the parking lot, right to the end of the revival, it was a time of miracles, rejoicing, and praise. As the days passed by my hunger and desire to serve the Lord grew. I attended as many prayer meetings as possible.

PASTOR TONY SIANSO, ASSEMBLY OF GOD

One Saturday morning I attended the Full Gospel Business Men's Fellowship International breakfast meeting. The guest speaker was a man named Tony Sianso. Tony was a customer of mine from my restaurant. When he heard that I was born again, he was overjoyed. He said, "Bruno, I have been praying for your salvation for five years, and I always prayed for myself for protection before I would enter your restaurant, because I knew you were in the Mafia and a dangerous man."

Tony, who was a Pastor from the Assemblies of God denomination, invited me to a small outreach in Anaheim that he was preparing. He asked me to work with him. I accepted his offer and for the next 6 months I began to feed the homeless and reach out to the alcoholics and drug addicts. We saw many miracles manifested and people saved during this time. This was a glorious time for me to be helping others and to be with Pastor Tony. He was a man of great compassion and a great soul winner. He was a good friend, a good brother in the Lord. He taught me much about the pastoral gifts and pastoral anointing. He was the first person to encourage me and allow me to preach at a Sunday church service. I was so excited by this opportunity that I was awake for two nights straight preparing the message. During these 6 months I was traveling back and forth between Anaheim, California, and Bullhead City, Arizona, where I owned property. This is where I originally had planned to live and build my 'Casino'. After much prayer the Lord showed me that He wanted me to stay in Bullhead City for a time. I did not immediately understand why, but the Lord's leading was very clear and strong. So much so, that He opened a door and permitted me to buy a brand new three bedroom house on top of a mountain overlooking the Colorado River and all the casinos on the other side of the river, in Laughlin, Nevada. From my house, I could see for miles up and down the river, and I could see Laughlin and all the casinos in that area. Within thirty days, my home and business in California were sold. God definitely had a plan! He was working powerfully again in my life and was preparing something special. I did not know then, but God was getting ready to use me and was setting me apart for a ministry of prayer and fasting. When God moves in your life just follow Him. Because He has done a good work in you. (See Ephesians 2:10) I began packing my things from the house in California for the move to Arizona. Early Sunday morning, during my devotion, I was praying for my church, 'Melodyland'. I was asking the Lord for more confirmation about this move. I really liked my church and it was difficult for me to leave the congregation and my friends. 'Melodyland' was also one of the leading churches and Schools of Theology in Southern California at that time. The Pastor of the church, Ralph Wilkerson, was a great man of God. As I was praying and interceding for 'Melodyland' that morning, the Lord gave me a vision. I saw Pastor Wilkerson in the Spirit and he looked like an angel. I did not understand and was startled by the vision. At the church service, everything became clear to me.

During the praise and worship at church, everyone experienced the glory of God coming down, and the manifestation of the Holy Spirit was moving in a mighty way. All of a sudden everyone became completely quiet and still. Then the Pastor began to prophesy. In his prophecy he said, "There is someone here who is going to the mountains. You think it is the end, but it is only the beginning, thus saith the Lord." Then I saw the Lord in a bright light standing in front of me. It was as if the Lord came to me from His shepherd, Pastor Wilkerson. I knew that it was the confirmation of my prayer request about the move. I had never mentioned my thoughts about moving to Arizona to Pastor Wilkerson. The Lord is faithful and answers prayer! That afternoon and all night I finished packing and headed off to Arizona.

12
VISITATION OF ANGELS

After several hours of driving through the desert, I was getting tired and sleepy. I pulled off the road into a rest area. No sooner had I stopped the rented truck and turned off the engine, than I fell immediately into a deep sleep. During the night I awoke and looked at my watch. It was 4:00 a.m. I did not know where I was or who I was. It was as if I had lost my identity. Fear filled me. I thought, "What am I doing?" I sold my business, I'm in a rented truck with all of my furniture and belongings, and I'm headed for an uncertain future. I felt literally lost in the desert! I felt just like Moses and the Hebrews in their exodus from Egypt. I felt a strong desire to go back to 'Melodyland'. To all the people and friends, and to all that was so familiar to me. Just as I thought these things, I saw two angels in front of me about 50 feet away. They were in mid-air, approximately 25 feet above the ground. They called to me. They said, "Bruno, come follow us, come follow us." They waved to me to go forward with them. The sense of my identity came back to me. I felt awake, alert, clear minded and fresh. I was ready to go again! I started the truck and drove off following the angels toward my destination. I have been following angels and the Holy Spirit ever since.

Psalms 103:20-22, "Bless the Lord, ye his angels, that excel in strength, that do his commandments, hearkening unto the voice of his word. Bless ye the Lord, all ye his hosts; ye ministers of his that do his pleasure. Bless the Lord, all his works in all places of his dominion: bless the Lord, O my soul."

Also in Hebrews 1:14, it says,
Are they not all ministering spirits, sent forth to minister for them who shall be heirs of salvation?

God is faithful to everyone who believes in Christ Jesus. God puts His angels around all who have received His Son. You can know, now, that even though you might be in a low point of your life. Going through trials and tribulations, including doubting your salvation and the calling on your life. You can experience what I experienced. What the people in the Bible experienced when they left Egypt in their exodus with Moses. They experienced the presence of angels and the glory of the Holy Spirit. The Bible says that 2.5 million people experienced the glory of God manifested in the congregation while they were camped in the desert. His glory and His fire filled and illuminated every area of their lives. It was their guide. Everyone saw the glory of the Lord in the cloud and in the fire. How much more does the Lord have for you and me in the glory of His resurrected Son, Jesus Christ? In His Holy Spirit, to fill us and guide us? (See Exodus 40:34-38) I had been driving for several hours and I would soon be reaching the Arizona border. While I was driving, I was singing songs to the Lord and looking at the stars above shining at me. I was so full of joy that I began to sing prayers, in song, to the Lord, "I want more of You, I want more of Your Holy Spirit, I want more of You, heavenly Father, I want to be like Your Son, Jesus." I kept praying to the Lord and confessing, "Thank You Lord for sending your angels to lead me. Thank You for your angels to confirm your plan for me. Thank You Lord for selling my house and business. Thank You Lord for giving me a house in the mountains." I was overjoyed with God's reality. With my singing and praying and total absorption in the Lord, I finally reached Arizona early in the morning. It seemed like I didn't even realize the distance or the burden of the journey. I knew beyond a shadow of a doubt that I was determined. With every fiber of my being, I wanted to seek and follow the Lord. He was becoming a consuming fire of joy for me.

I remembered an incident back at 'Melodyland' in Anaheim. Oral Roberts was the invited speaker for the evening. He said that everyone God calls into leadership Ministry He will direct to fast and pray. To seek this high calling. He continued that, "God will also cloister his called ones to the mountains for this purpose." We read in Galatians 2:1 how the Lord, after baptizing Paul in the Holy Spirit, took him to the mountains. He also took Moses to the mountains. He took His disciples to the mountains. It was now becoming very clear to me what God was doing to me. It was overwhelming as I realized the significance of the house on the mountain that God had given to me. To begin this new journey of my life, to enter a new land, and to be led to a mountain, was so awesome. A flooding joy was filling me beyond my imagination. My mind was being consumed with only thoughts of the Lord and His Word. Thoughts of his desires concerning people, and His unexplainable joys and victories in every way imaginable for those who come to know him. I recalled at that moment that the Bible declares in Philippians 3:13-14,

> Brethren, I count not myself to have apprehended: but this one thing I do, forgetting those things which are behind, and reaching forth unto those things which are before, I press toward the mark for the prize of the high calling of God in Christ Jesus.

As I began to unload the truck at my new house, I was tired from the journey. I felt that I needed to rest and pray. I took my mattress and a few blankets out of the truck and put them down in the living room. I knelt on the mattress to pray. Instantly, I felt a warmth come over me as if a heavy blanket of love was beginning to cover my shoulders and my body. It was such a pleasant feeling. Words cannot describe what it was like, but I know now what happened. In a moment, the Holy Spirit illuminated the room, my mind and my whole being. While I was there worshipping the Lord, I fell asleep. I had a vision. In it I saw the glory and the fire of the Lord coming down, and I heard the voice of God. It was an audible voice that called to me and He said, "Bruno, Bruno my son, it is I the Lord your God." I responded, "Yes, Lord." Then the Lord said, "Ask me anything and I will give it to you." I said, "Lord, I only want to worship you." I had the most wonderful nights sleep in my life that night. The scripture that comes to mind is Deuteronomy 5:23-24:

Dr. Bruno Caporrimo

> And it came to pass, when ye heard the voice out of the midst of the darkness, (for the mountain did burn with fire,) that ye came near unto me, even all the heads of your tribes, and your elders; And ye said, Behold, the Lord our God hath shewed us his glory and his greatness, and we have heard his voice out of the midst of the fire: we have seen this day that God doth talk with man, and he liveth.

Dear friends, I hope this will encourage you and inspire you to seek the Lord and the calling He has for your life. He has the answer for all your needs. He is just waiting for you to seek Him and ask. I will now share with you, dear reader, the impact, transformation and manifestation of my Honeymoon with the Holy Spirit from 1986 to 1991. I hope the major incidents of these years will touch and inspire you to grab hold of the powerful truths that the Lord has for your life. What I share is for all who seek Him, not for just a select few. Several days went by and I was totally unpacked. I put all the literature I had collected and saved and brought with me in one of the rooms of my house. By this time in my Christian experience, I had accumulated many Christian books from great men and women of God. Evangelists like Morris Cerullo, Billy Graham, Oral Roberts, Roberts Lairdon, Smith Wigglesworth, and many others. I thank the Lord for giving me those books. I also had many Christian Gospel tracts. I had a selection of just about all the tracts available on the subjects of gambling, drinking, drugs, etc. because I knew the Lord had prepared me and was giving me a burden for the lost souls in the casinos. My past life as a professional gambler was now going to be used mightily for the glory of God, hallelujah! I was determined and ready to go invade the casinos and flood them with Christian tracts to help snatch the people there from the deception they lived in, under the hand of Satan. At that time, I made a vow to the Lord that in addition to reading the Bible, I would fast and pray three days a week. I wanted to do this because I knew there were many things I still did not know about our triune God. So I wanted to know more! All these plans were now possible to consider because the Lord sold my house and restaurant. I had enough money in the bank for about 5 years. I could literally dedicate my life full-time to God, His Son, and the Holy Spirit. This was yet another miracle in the magnificent plans of an omnipotent God!

THE EXPERIENCE OF FASTING AND PRAYER

The Bible declares in Matthew that when we fast, we should anoint ourselves with oil and fast in secret. (See Matthew 6:17-18) That is what I did. I began to spend my time reading the Bible several hours a day and I would literally go into a closet in the house during this time to fast and pray and intercede in prayer for the casinos across the river in Nevada. I prayed for all the ministries that I had come in contact with in my life. I prayed that God would birth through them a five fold ministry. (See Ephesians 4:11) If you would follow this example, I believe the glory of God, as I experienced in that closet, will manifest in full measure in your life. I followed the example found in Matthew 6:6,

> But thou, when thou prayest, enter into thy closet, and when thou hast shut thy door, pray to thy Father which is in secret; and thy Father which seeth in secret shall reward thee openly.

It was now 1986. Now that I am settled in my new home, I find myself with no reputation. I did not know any big ministries. I had no schedules or bookings. I was not a famous preacher even though, for the last 12 months, I had experienced many miracles. I had a visitation from the Lord. No one knew me, but I knew in my heart that He called me to the nations. That he called me to be a World Evangelist. I watched all the famous Evangelists. I knew I wanted to preach, small church, large church, I did not know how or when, but I knew the time would come for me. I found myself up in the mountains and I knew the hand of the Lord had carried me this far. I had forsaken all my family and old friends. I do not believe anyone knew I existed except for the Lord. I began to understand that God was setting the stage for my life in this time and season. The only purpose for this building of character in me was because He knew best. He knew that I was not ready to go to the nations. He was building character in me and in my heart; breaking some obstacles like pride, anger, bitterness and rejection. I found myself wanting to love and seek God more. Although He was breaking me, the love and hunger for him grew stronger. I wanted more. I was not satisfied. I wanted to spread what I had. Keeping the experience all to myself would be a sin. I wanted to reach those souls in the casinos. I wanted to reach those souls more than anything and tell them that the person I was honeymooning with, the Messiah, could be much greater than gambling, smoking, drinking, and the opposite sex. I wept for their souls and I started fasting and praying that the Lord would anoint me to go into the casinos and proclaim the gospel. This was my focus. My single goal at that time. I began to understand God's plan for my life. How he had filled me, and delivered me with His Spirit, from gambling, smoking and drinking. He had given me this beautiful home looking down at the casino and river. The first week I knelt down and anointed myself with oil and vowed to the Father that I would not eat anything. That I would only drink water. I would love to share with you what I had week after week. I did not plan to fast every week. I only vowed to fast for three days. I heard many Bible teachers say that if you fast for three days, the Lord would give you spiritual muscles. My soul longed for the anointing. I so wanted to be used by the Lord. I wanted to cast out devils, heal the sick and bring souls into God's Kingdom.

ELEMENTS OF FASTING

I did not tell anyone I was fasting and reading the Bible two hours every day. I went to the closet and prayed for my needs first. I prayed for strength for my needs and the needs of others. I began to intercede for the nations. I started bombarding heaven for all the casinos in the area. This took me two hours a day which seemed like ten minutes. The time seemed to go by very fast because God was in it. I began to enjoy the breakthrough of intercession in prayer. I would worship the Lord an hour and a half every day. I would put my special tape of worship and praise songs on. This tape was put together by Bill Bright. It was old Psalms songs that came from the Bible. It included hymns like, 'Majesty', and 'Thou Art Worthy.' As I began to worship I found myself on the floor every day with a blanket on my head. You would ask, "Pastor Bruno, why a blanket over your head?" I wanted to be in the dark with no distractions. I would do this day after day. The results were supernatural. The power of God started to move through the house. All the gifts of the Holy Spirit were manifested in my life.

I found rest, peace and complete fulfillment every day. I felt secure. There was no fear or worry. Through praise and worship, I realized I was in the perfect will of God. Where He would put His arms around me and love me as a husband loves his bride. There I began to discern and to hear the voice of the Lord in the still quietness. I did this for three days. On the third and final day I prepared myself to go out. I found myself for the next four days going to casinos. I passed out 5,000 tracts to anyone that I could. That was the most wonderful week of my life. Thirty people came to the Lord. They were snatched from hell. I had to be very careful with the security guards because I was told that witnessing in the casino was soliciting and against the law. Anyone caught in the casino preaching the gospel would be arrested with a misdemeanor charge. That Sunday I took inventory of what occurred during the week and the experiences I felt in my life. I knew that the Lord had given me thirty souls. I knew it was because of the Lord's anointing that the people came to Christ. John 6:44 says, "No man can come to me, except the Father which hath sent me draw him: and I will raise him up at the last day." I was excited. I prepared to fast another three days. I knew that the power of God was with me in those three days. Within those three days I found myself resting in the Lord, fasting, reading the Bible and quality Christian books. Each day I experienced the fullness of the Holy Spirit. At the end of the third day, I was so full, I was not hungry at all. Also, reader, each day you fast for the Lord you lose two pounds. At the end of this fast I found myself healthier, slimmer and in the fullness of His wonderful love. I felt that the gifts were flowing in me and I experienced the sweet anointing of the Holy Spirit in my mouth. It was sweeter than honey. I understood what the Bible meant in Psalms 34:8 and Ezekiel 3:3,

> O taste and see that the Lord is good: blessed is the man that trusteth in him.

> And he said unto me, Son of man, cause thy belly to eat, and fill thy bowels with this roll that I give thee. Then did I eat it; and it was in my mouth as honey for sweetness.

13
WITNESS AND PASS OUT TRACTS IN CASINOS

It was an awesome experience to drool with the sweetness of God. For the first time I realized that Moses, the Israelites, King David, and all of God's people in the Bible, had experienced this. On Wednesday night, the third day of the second fast experience, I remembered telling the Lord that I wanted to meet some friends and meet some churches in the area. That night I found myself going to a small Assembly of God church in the City of Riviera. The majority of the members worked in the casinos. The Lord gave me favor and within the next five years, I worked with the Pastor doing street outreach. On Thursday, Friday, Saturday and Sunday, after my devotion with the Lord, I would go to different casinos to witness and pass out tracts.

I would like to share with you my strategies. Firstly I was always well dressed. Secondly, my conduct with people always included smiling, reading the people, and making contact with a friendly conversation. Thirdly, I would go inside the casinos and put literature and tracts everywhere possible. This included the slot machines, men's rooms, inside menus, and I tried to contain myself. I tried to not be too radical and to not make any commotion. Many people, either one on one or in small groups, confessed Jesus Christ. I led them in the sinner's prayer for the first time in their lives. Afterwards, I prepared myself to fast again.

Each room in my home was like a library. I read five books a week and listened to a lot of teaching tapes.

I had a friend in the city who was my partner before I was a Christian. We had planned to build a casino together. That was his ultimate goal. My friend had lived in Bullhead City, Arizona, for many years. He was well established and owned a hotel and a construction company. Prior to coming to the Lord, I had spent many years with my friend and his darling wife, Anita. Joe Calucci was very calm and very sensible. I was fasting and praying for my friend Joe. That he would accept the new me and my Jesus. After fasting, one afternoon, I went out preaching and passing out tracts in all the casinos.

After I had been witnessing in the casinos for several months, Joe and his wife invited me to dinner. That night after dinner my friend questioned me, "What has gotten hold of you? You are a changed man. You are radical. We were planning to build a casino together and now you are different. People are complaining about you, that you are too radical. The word is out in the casinos that they want to eliminate you because you are taking their business and talking about this Jesus." Joe explained, "We love you and want to protect you, we don't want you to get killed. My wife and I will send you to college but you must stop preaching and passing out tracts around the casinos. If you want to preach, go to college and be normal. Preach inside a building. Stay off the streets. My wife and I are willing to pay all expenses for four years because we want the best for you." I knew that was a wonderful gesture on their part, since I had not had a college education. I was very moved by their kindness. I rejected the offer because I knew in my heart that He was sending me to the streets and the casinos at this present time. I replied to Anita and Joe, "Thank you for your wonderful offer, and I know you love me. I would like to ask you to do me a favor." They both responded, "Sure, anything." "Joe, if I were to die tomorrow, I would go to heaven. Joe, would you like to be there with me?" My old friend in crime and his wife responded, "Yes." I led both of them in the sinner's prayer. Hallelujah!

Right there and then I had no regrets for rejecting the college offer. I knew that the best school was a relationship and honeymoon with the Holy Ghost. He would be my teacher and out of this relationship, I would be compelled to go into the highways and by-ways. Also, I knew by the Spirit that it was not my friends offering this school but the god of this world, to side-track me from my calling. To eliminate me from God's perfect will. The time was not right. It was a snare planned by satan. Week after week I went from casino to casino. In this city there were 33 churches, including Jehovah Witnesses, Mormon and Catholic. I visited every one of them and worked with many of them. In fast after fast, I would spend my time learning how to be more effective. How to reach more people for the Lord. Encounters with the police came at the beginning of 1987. I remember an experience from my days with the casinos.

After fasting I went there to have lunch. The casinos have the best lunches. I witnessed to a waitress. A Spanish lady named Margarita. When she came to Christ she asked me for a Spanish Bible. The following day, after my worship with the Lord, I again experienced a tremendous and powerful anointing that God released into my spirit. I rejoiced because of it. I would like to tell you what I have discovered on a one on one basis. I want to share something that you can experience in your own home. When you worship the Lord in your home, the Lord will release the resurrection power of the Holy Spirit in your life. Whether you are a full time minister or not you are able to adopt this pattern of one-on-one worship in your home. You will experience the great manifestation of the resurrection power of the Holy Spirit. Then you can go out and deliver this anointing to whoever wants it. As you study the life of David, the beloved of God, you see that every time he was in trouble, every time he was struggling, he went to worship God. (See Psalms 34:1-3) Whether he was in a cave, a building, or in the open. David the shepherd boy, even when he was 13 years old, knew how to have a breakthrough in his life and to be empowered by the Holy Spirit. Afterwards, he would go forward and fight the battle of the Lord. The Holy Spirit never leaves you. He abides in you forever. In 1 Samuel 16:1-13, Samuel the prophet is instructed by the Lord to anoint David king to be. The Lord said to Samuel,

> How long wilt thou mourn for Saul, seeing I have rejected him from reigning over Israel? Fill thine horn with oil, and go, I will send thee to Jesse the Bethlehemite: for I have provided me a king among his sons....Then Samuel took the horn of oil, and

anointed him in the midst of his brethren: and the Spirit of the LORD came upon David from that day forward. So Samuel rose up, and went to Ramah.

The Lord Jesus tells us in the book of John that the Holy Spirit promised by God was not only for that day. (See John 14:16) Not only does the Holy Spirit come and abide in you forever but He empowers you for service. To bring revival everywhere you go. The Lord has called me to bring His presence to God's people everywhere I go. While I was getting ready to go back into the casino, I was looking for a Spanish Bible for Margarita. I felt like a million dollars. I was ready to go out and bless someone. As I entered the casino that afternoon, I looked for Margarita. She was off that day. I walked around this particular casino. I started walking toward the bowling alley on the North side of the casino. There was a couple there that were drinking and fighting. I approached them boldly and gave them a tract and told them, "Jesus loves you." The man was startled and gave me a dirty look and continued his argument with the woman. As I walked away, I plead the blood of Jesus over that place. I started interceding in prayer. I started taking authority over Satan. My prayer was very simple, "Father, in Jesus name, I lift up this casino to you and I plead the blood of Jesus over it. Right now, Lord, I ask for Michael the Angel to come forth to cast out every demonic influence from this casino. I pray that the Holy Spirit will invade this building, every person, every heart, soul and mind, in Jesus name." I walked toward the buffet lounge and sat down and ate my lunch. There were about 500 people eating there. The people were from all over the world; California, England, China, Europe. I was in the Laughlin Casino. Don Laughlin was the owner of this casino. He owned not only the casino, but the entire city.

He began this in a small town. When he started, it was full of miners and cowboys. That was in 1918. Seventy years had passed and he turned this city into an empire. I pray that Don Laughlin would become born again. So here I am in this casino. I was the only Evangelist bringing God to the lost souls. The reason why I bring this to your attention is because, whenever the church has condemned gambling, drinking or prostitution, the gambling industry and all the stock holders have come against the ministers of the gospel. They have a reputation in the past of burning churches down or running them out of town. Here I am, among this crowd, and I'm smiling at people and trying to have a conversation with them. In a matter of seconds I take out my literature and tracts and distribute them to as many people as possible. People received me because I was dressed well and they were expecting to get something for free. They assumed I was giving them coupons to gamble. They never expected that I was a minister of the gospel and that what they were about to receive was life instead of death. I sat down and watched them read their tracts. I allowed a few moments to go by and then I started conversations with the people around me about the Lord. This was very effective. The people felt the acceptance and the love of the Lord Jesus, and the anointing of the Holy Spirit. While I was preaching and talking to the people I noticed a waitress with an evil look. She was the one substituting for Margarita. She ran out of the room and suddenly the Holy Spirit spoke to me. I heard the sweet voice of the Holy Spirit telling me to leave now. I disobeyed the Holy Spirit and stayed 10 minutes longer.

I began to debate with a Jewish man. I went back to the bowling alley to minister to the couple that were arguing. I noticed they had left. I began to walk by the bowling alley and I put tracts on everything possible. People were drinking and smoking. When I reached the end of the building, to my surprise, as I looked down the bowling alley there appeared two security officers looking straight at me. They gestured with their finger for me to come with them. When I reached them I noticed that they had every piece of literature that I had passed out. Their hands were full. The tracts in their possession were specifically made to expose the evils of gambling, drinking and prostitution. They looked at me and screamed, "Are you responsible for this?" I answered, "Yes Sir." They advised me, "You are not allowed to do this. You are soliciting in the casino." I responded, "Do you see that badge that you have on? We work for the same boss." Instantly the female officer points her finger at me and says, "You are not allowed to do this here. You are under ...." Suddenly her mouth froze. I knew she wanted to say that I was under arrest but she could not say it. She continued to point her finger at me with authority. I responded, "I'm leaving." The Holy Spirit intervened and saved my life. They escorted me through the bowling alley, the lounge, down the casino and out the door. Two angels disguised as security guards escorted me. I knew they were operating in the spirit of error and had fallen victims to the god of this world. As we went through the swinging doors and outside I turned around and said, "God bless you." Instantly the woman changed and was convicted by the Holy Spirit. She answered, "Please forgive me. I am Christian too. Please come back when I am not on duty to witness." I want to emphasize that the Holy Spirit protected me from going to jail by closing the mouth of the security guard and allowing them to escort me outside to safety and then apologize to me. I had V.I.P. treatment. These are some of the results of honeymooning with the Holy Spirit. The scripture that comes to my mind is, Matthew 28:19-20,

> Go ye therefore, and teach all nations, baptizing them in the name of the Father, and of the Son, and of the Holy Ghost: Teaching them to observe all things whatsoever I have commanded you: and, lo, I am with you always, even unto the end of the world.

God is faithful. I rejoice that Jesus and the Holy Spirit and the Father are faithful to deliver their manifestations and power, to see you through your time of need, if you only believe. Another scripture that comes to mind and is appropriate is Matthew 10:16-20,

> Behold, I send you forth as sheep in the midst of wolves: be ye therefore wise as serpents, and harmless as doves. But beware of men: for they will deliver you up to the councils, and they will scourge you in their synagogues; And ye shall be brought before governors and kings for my sake, for a testimony against them and the Gentiles. But when they deliver you up, take no thought how or what ye shall speak: for it shall be given you in that same hour what ye shall speak. For it is not ye that speak, but the Spirit of your Father which speaketh in you.

After being warned by the security officers, I began to change my strategy. Now I was witnessing in the parking lot. Bill Bright says that 60% of the people who come to Christ do so by reading tracts.

I continued witnessing in the parking lot and on street corners near the casinos. There were people everywhere as is the tradition in casino cities. The tourists are always willing to receive literature. I remember disguising myself in an Army special forces uniform one time. The jacket had special pockets for many tracts to be carried. I would disguise myself in order not to be questioned or arrested by casino security. My favorite spot was between casinos.

Many tourists would pass them when going from one casino to another. From there I could see people who felt disgusted and bored. Unhappy losers who lost their money and were looking to get something for free. I would say to the people, "If you get this you will hit the real jackpot." I would find myself with people from all over taking tracts from me. If you know anything about casino cities you know that the gamblers walk around with buckets that look like Kentucky Fried Chicken buckets. I would drop the tracts into their buckets. Some believed these were coupons for something free. Some would say, "I am a Christian". Others would answer, "I needed that." Still others would throw them on the floor. One of the reasons why I told them to read and receive it and win the jackpot, was because my intention was that they would receive Jesus Christ and begin their honeymoon with the Holy Spirit. I would like to share with you my militancy and determination to reach the lost in the casinos. Many people have asked me why I do this. The reason is because I have love for lost souls. When I came from Italy as a teenager I fell into the trap of satan. He made me believe that gambling and drinking were okay. By listening to the enemies lies I became a professional gambler and loser for twenty years. I began to play poker as a young teenager in New York City. I got involved with the nightclubs and the underworld, and slowly I was promoted by satan to go into heavy gambling. I was flying back and forth, year after year, to Las Vegas. Now that I belong to the right master and have been transformed by the hand of the Messiah, I want to give him equal time and all my time to bring people from destruction and darkness to the light. From satan to God.

The following night the casinos were having special celebrities. People were coming in with Rolls Royce cars and Limousines. I was standing there with my best suit on when a very elegant lady got out of a limousine and leaned towards me and smiled. I smiled back and said, "Good evening". She asked me," What do you do?" I answered, "My father owns everything around here." I gave her a tract. She looked at me and ripped up my tract and threw it in my face. Her comment to me was, "This is what I think of your Jesus." She walked away with extreme pride into the casino.

The next Sunday I went to Calvary Chapel. The pastor and his wife were very devoted ministers to the lost. On Sunday nights they would go by the river below the casinos, where many people were stranded after losing all their money. We would take food and drinks to the homeless by the river. While I was going down the line I noticed there was a lady with her hands covering her face as if trying to hide from me. I reached to give her a sandwich and with shame in her face she said, "Thank you, you do not recognize me?" I responded, "No." She said in tears, "I am the lady who ripped up the flyer and threw it in your face three days ago." She continued her story. She said that she had gambled away all her wealth and her husband told her, "Do not come home." She began to cry. I sensed the power of God's conviction in this precious woman. She explained, "I lost everything. I have been a gambler for over twenty years. I also lost my marriage." She asked, "Why would God do this to me?" I looked at her in her eyes and said, "God did not do this to you. Satan and society did this to you. Satan and society deceived you. Gambling is contrary to the laws of God. Gambling goes under the category of idolatry and is witchcraft." She looked at me and exclaimed, "I did not know that." I responded, "Yes. Only Jesus can change you. I believe now is the time and the Lord has brought you here to tell you that He loves you. He wants to come into your heart and has a plan for your life. Would you like that?"

While tears were coming down her face she said, "Yes I want Jesus." Hallelujah! My coworker and I knelt beside her and presented her to the Lord Jesus Christ. Suddenly I looked up and saw the bright lights of Arizona. Everything was bright and full of life. I remember saying, "Thank you Holy Spirit. You make everything so beautiful." I watched this precious lady eating her sandwich and her face shining up with fullness of joy. We spent thirty minutes reading scripture to her. She was full of questions. I read her a passage from Exodus 20:17, "Thou shalt not covet thy neighbour's house, thou shalt not covet thy neighbour's wife, nor his manservant, nor his maidservant, nor his ox, nor his ass, nor any thing that is thy neighbours." The Hebrew and Greek definition for "covet" is to; violate the privacy of their possession. When people violate the laws of God they are manipulated and deceived into falsity, unjustness and greed. The word "greed" is categorized with the words for demonology, evil, concupiscence and covetousness, which is idolatry. Idolatry is demonology which brings a demonic influence into someone's life to cause a harmful addiction. So that that person will stray from God. If you would like to know more about this subject please read, "The Invisible War".

I would like to share with you that in America alone there are 18 million people that are trying to recover from gambling addictions. This report was given in 2000 from the gambler's anonymous organization. This huge number does not include people in places such as Monte Carlo or Italy. China alone has 200 million gambling addicts. What the nations of the world need is Jesus Christ. There are many denominations that compromise the gospel and say that it is okay to gamble. The lie is that you can keep it in moderation. If you ask anyone who is a professional gambler how they started, they will tell you that it all began in their living room or at a sociable card club. Even the lottery is an aspect of witchcraft, idolatry and covetousness. There is no such thing as legal gambling. The bible is very clear that an honest day's work brings an honest day's pay. By the way, could this be you? If you have any of these symptoms, now is the time to take an inventory of yourself and stop and do what I did. Call upon the Lord Jesus Christ. He will come and visit you right now. Give all your addictions to the Holy Spirit and he will give you comfort, peace and joy. My only purpose for writing this book is to expose the enemy and bring the pure gospel and the wonderful Holy Spirit to people's lives. Maybe you picked up this book in the bookstore or somebody gave it to you and you like what I'm writing. I hope that you continue to read this book to the end. I hope that you find comfort and joy in identifying yourself to my testimony. You can cry out to God. Don't give up because you don't know what life can bring to you tomorrow. Your tomorrow is in God and only He can give you peace and destiny and the dream beyond. He offers much greater than what life can offer. Life is not fair but God is good.

14
TRAGEDY AND DISAPPOINTMENT COMING MY WAY, BUT NEVER DEFEATED

I remember, it was 1987, and I was continuing to be a witness in the casino. I was trying to encourage and inspire Angela to work together with me. She responded that it was not very popular to pass out tracks or witness in the casino area. She had responded very well for several years but now she was losing faith. She insisted that she go out and get a job. Two dear friends, Joe and Anita Colucci, were having a grand opening of their small restaurant and pizza shop. They were more than willing and very happy to give Angela a job. We told them it would be only for two years because we were waiting for God's instructions. They were very excited and they made Angela manager. She worked until late at night so I would have time to study the scriptures and grow in the Lord as I was learning to do greater outreach. Two years went by, three years went by, four years went by and I watched Angela become lukewarm. She began to gamble, because the pizza shop had slot machines, and come home late. I began to fast and pray for her and remind her that God raised her from the dead, that she should be humble and grateful and be committed to the things of God. She responded to me by saying, "Hey, we've been here five years. There is no money coming in and I don't think that God can do anything for us." I reminded her that if we would be faithful that God would promote us. I told her that we could travel and have a great ministry. I continued to be stronger and stronger by seeking the Lord day after day, moment after moment. Angela grew weaker and weaker. We were having less conversation. She would work during the night and she would sleep during the day. I began to feel that my marriage was losing ground and I felt that we needed counseling.

One Sunday afternoon, at 5 p.m., we went into the shopping center near one of the large casinos where the pizza shop was located. I was coming off a three day fast and I got the idea to do an outreach in front of the pizza shop. A funny thing happened. Angela was serving beer and managing the gambling machines, while I was passing out gospel tracts to people. Many people were coming out from a drinking bash and I was there witnessing to repent and lead them to Christ. The whole thing seemed comical. Angela was feeding them fleshly desire and I was trying to give them spiritual drink. There was a war going on in the spirit. I hope that you get what I mean. Joe Colucci, the owner of the pizza shop came by and said, "What's the matter with you? Why are you telling people about the Lord? Are you trying to destroy my business?" So you see, at one time he was my best friend, but now that I am a witness for Christ he became my enemy. Angela was becoming hard-hearted towards me. The scripture came to my mind, "My people perish for lack of knowledge." As I walked away and turned around the corner, suddenly, someone tapped me on my shoulder. I turned around and this large man of about 6'9" was standing there. He said to me, "I know who you are, Bruno. Do not come around the mobile home park anymore. You bring shame to me by preaching the Gospel to everyone." I felt fear for a moment and my knees were shaking. I then looked at him and said, "You know Satan is a liar." He responded, "No I am God." I remembered that the week before that I did an outreach in the mobile-park on the other side of town. Many, many, people responded except this Goliath man. When I knocked on his door he came out very arrogantly and he belittled me. He told me, "Get out of here and don't come back here anymore". Now this 6'9"Goliath man is looking down on me. He looked at the bible and said, "You are a Christian. If anyone asks you for anything, you need to give it to them." I nodded my head and said yes. He replied, "I want your shirt." I did something that I would have never done before. In the past, I would probably have beat his neck off. But now I am a child of God. I had been saved more than five years and I admit I felt nervous and fearful. I looked him in his eyes and I compromised. Gently I took my shirt and gave to him. It had many flowers and beautiful colors. I gave it to him. In my frustration, I admit, that fear got a hold of me. I did not know what to do. I walked away thinking, "I need to pray and re-organize my thoughts." I went back to my car and headed home.

I went home to my prayer closet and started bombarding heaven and pulling down the strong-holds over the city. Once again the Holy Spirit began to anoint me. I asked the Lord to pull the fiery darts out of my body and I began to feel the strength of Samson come upon me. I felt strength and boldness come upon me. Immediately I went back to the parking lot to get back in my position and make a stand for the gospel. A lady from the pizza shop came out and told me that the man who had taken my shirt, had started vandalizing the cars in the parking lot. She continued that he wanted to know which vehicle belonged to me. That somebody had called the authorities and he had been arrested. I was also told that it took 4 to 5 police to apprehend him. I nodded in agreement and said to her, "You know that God is love and that man chooses not to love." As long as there are people who will decide not to love, we will need the police, the marines, navy, and the coast guard. God's law is to protect people that choose to love. To love is the first and foremost commandment and the second commandment is, to love your neighbor as you love yourself. God gives us the freedom to choose whether or not we're going to love. By the way, the Bible declares that the police are sent by the Lord."

> Romans 13:1-5: Let every soul be subject unto the higher powers. For there is no power but of God: the powers that be are ordained of God. Whosoever therefore resisteth the power, resisteth the ordinance of God: and they that resist shall receive to themselves damnation. For rulers are not a terror to good works, but to the evil. Wilt thou then not be afraid of the power? do that which is good, and thou shalt have praise of the same: For he is the minister of God to thee for good. But if thou do that which is evil, be afraid; for he beareth not the sword in vain: for he is the minister of God, a revenger to execute wrath

upon him that doeth evil. Wherefore ye must needs be subject, not only for wrath, but also for conscience sake.

I wish that the scripture above, I would have known before I got into the mafia. Then I could have been optimistic, to do the right thing. But now, my character has been built in the Lord Jesus Christ. Even though people are pessimistic, I can be optimistic. It is very unfortunate that this man refused to listen to the Gospel. He allowed himself to be a victim of Satan and wind up in jail. My prayer to the Lord is that God would give convicts his heart for repentance. That they will come to the knowledge of the Gospel and receive full deliverance. To obey the laws of the land, do what is right, and shun all evil. I pray they can come to the knowledge of the Holy Spirit and have a Honeymoon experience too. After speaking with the woman at the pizza shop and having the experience with Goliath, the Lord released a tremendous anointing and gave me great joy and liberty. In only 3 hours, I passed out over 3,000 tracts. I put them everywhere. On every doorknob and car. When people would ask me what motivated me to do all that, I responded, "I just love the Lord. I love to do it. I enjoy it." I believe it is fun to serve the Lord Jesus Christ. The Gospel is fun. The bible declares that the kingdom of God is love, joy, and peace. If you want to experience the fullness of joy in your life, ask the Holy Spirit to transform you in Jesus name. I hope you can have a Honeymoon with the Holy Spirit too!!

In 1991 I was praying and sending an e-mail to heaven, asking God if Angela would quit the job, so that we could serve the Lord together. Six months went by and Angela became very sick. That morning I remember she had made a phone call to Joe Colucci asking him to get a replacement because she was very, very, sick. She came down with a terrible cold. Joe responded, "What about my store. Who's going to open the store?" Angela said, "I'm very, very, sick. I've been faithful to your business for four years. I never took a day off and now that I am sick you are not concerned about my well being. You only care about your needs and your greed." She was very firm. She said, "Find yourself somebody else. I quit." I know that God answered my prayer. I was hoping that things would turn out for the good, but things got a little dramatic. A short time passed by and we closed the house down and moved back to Orange County. We managed to get a two bedroom apartment in Lake Elsinore. We found a Presbyterian Church and they welcomed us to work in the field reaching out to the homeless and gangs, to bring them to recovery. I made a contact with the local church in Orange County and the supermarket who supplied food for the events. Two days a week I picked up the food and distributed it to many locations like, 'Victory Outreach' or 'Set Free Ministry'. Financially, I had no income at all. There was no money coming in. Our budget was very tight and Angela was complaining and wanted to quit the ministry. I petitioned a telegram to Heaven and several days later the blessing came. I was given a very large conference room free of charge in one of the hotels in Buena Park. Because I was a ordained minister, I immediately made flyers. Three days a week I began to knock on the doors and pass these out to the people in the community. The response was good. People would say to me, "Yea, yea we'll come to your church." But the first Sunday morning there were only two people, me and my usher, who was in a wheelchair. He was there because he was a survivor from a plane crash and he was looking for a healing miracle.

Within six months we had more than forty-five people in the church. The majority of them were homeless, ex-gangsters and ex-drug addicts. They would come week after week. We would worship the Lord and the power of God would manifest every time. We experienced the transformation in people's lives. God gave me the compassion and the Love for lost souls. I remember the words of Jesus, "I have come for the sinners not for the righteous." A short time later God opened up a door and I had the honor and the privilege to meet Mariano and Anita Yo. They were Chinese missionaries from the Philippines living in Santa Ana, Ca. They conducted an outreach and maintained a mission home. Mariano invited me and Angela to work with him and live there. I was so impressed with these missionaries because they came from another country and were reaching the lost in America for Jesus.

Tragedy and disappointment approached me. Angela confronted me that she wanted to quit the ministry and give up our marriage. I did not accept it, instead, I went out and I began to work by picking avocados. I remember that, prior to coming to the Lord in the early 1970's, that I was raising money for the soccer team that I was coaching. I was getting more than ten-thousand dollars a year picking avocados from different peoples homes and selling them to the restaurant. The story began in

Dr. Bruno Caporrimo

1975. I had a very large avocado tree in my home. One afternoon I noticed that there were two guys on top of the wall picking the fruit. I remember parking the car and quietly approached these guys. I said to them, "Hey, what are you guy's doing?" One responded, "We're picking avocados." I said, "What are you going to do with them." He said, "Oh, we're 'gonna sell them, three for a dollar." My response was, "Let me buy fifty dollars worth." They rushed and within ten minutes, they had picked over two boxes of avocados. One of them came down saying to me, "Here's your avocados give us the money?" I said, "You're right these are my avocados. This is my tree and this is my house." I showed him my license and these two young men responded, "Please don't call the police." After I warned them I took all the avocados into my restaurant. I went back home with the soccer team, picked all the avocados within two hours, sold them to the restaurant and got 1,007 dollars. Wow! This is the way I raised up money for the soccer team.

Now I am in the ministry and I need to raise up money because the members of my church were very poor. I remember praying on my knees to the Lord this way, "God, if you bless me I will give ten percent of my income to Mariano and Anita, the missionaries." God blessed me. I began making more than two-thousand dollars a week picking and selling avocados. I would take my two-hundred dollar tithe, which is ten percent, and I would go to the mission home. I remember one afternoon I knocked on the door, a few seconds later the door opened and this young Chinese lady looked at me strange. I gave her the envelope and I said, "This money is from God to your papa." Angela was taking a different turn, to where my life and her life were changing forever. She was not impressed with what I was doing. She was not responding. Here I am working, our bills are paid, I am starting a church but my marriage was going in different directions. I began to fast and pray for the woman that I had loved for more than twenty years. I wanted to have a good marriage because I felt that together we could conquer the world and have a great ministry. The more I prayed the worse she got. I confronted her and she confessed that she had another man. We'll call him Dick. I remember that this man was married and that he was from India. He claimed to be a Christian and he wanted us to be involved in a multi-level with them. I rejected the offer but Angela continued the relationship with him. One night Angela told me he was going to

Laughlin Nevada and she asked me if she could go with them for five days to a vacation home. I replied, "Okay, they seem to be a nice couple, they are Christians."

When she came back home from the trip she looked terrible. Her countenance fell. I knew something was wrong. She said, "Oh no, I'm all right." Then, after several days I spent one night with this couple. The night of his wife's birthday. That is when I found out that he was in five religions. Dick was involved in Buddhism, Hinduism, Islam, Christianity and Scientology. When I confronted him with the Gospel he resisted me and he told me that all religions are good. Angela took a stand for him. That night, when we got home, I confronted Angela. She confessed that she was involved in a sexual relationship with him and soul tied to him. I found out that he brainwashed her mind and was controlling her. He took advantage of her. I tried day after day telling Angela that I loved her and that I forgave her and that it was okay. I told her that God loved her and so did I. I also suggested marriage counseling for us. She declined. She knew that I did not deserve this. She knew that I was faithful to God and to her. I could not bear to see my marriage breaking up. Dear reader, destruction, disappointment, and interruption can be expected during the long process of living out your life and dreams. When downtimes come and when your early enthusiasm diminishes and sometimes disappears. When energy-draining frustrations occur in the process, you need to stay focused. Dig in. Never quit. Hold on. I never gave up even though my marriage was finished. I never gave up. I remember that I was the one that made the vow to the Lord. I told him that if He brought Angela back from the dead, that I would serve him all the way. Time and again you may suffer from the loss of relationship. That is vital to your career. Not all of your trustful and helpful colleagues will remain at your side. Not even your spouse. Some may die and others will not be on the same page with you or your dream. They will slip away. Then unexpected problems arise, arguments and disagreements happen. Obstacles and obstructions emerge.

Sometimes the early excitement of your powerful Mission diminishes with time but you must stay focused. How do you handle the down times? When your enthusiasm begins to lose momentum? Pick-up the theme and vision of your dream and the possibility thinking creed: "I will not quit!" Pump the positive spirit by going to the window of your soul at the beginning of the day. Look at the new sunrise and affirm out loud, "This is the day that the Lord has made I will rejoice and I believe, I believe, and I believe and be glad in it". Do it faithfully, daily, and regularly! Affirm it as you put your head on the pillow at the end of the day. Stay focused on the dream. This is my testimony. I have been there for twenty years. This is the report of my research. This is a true story of how God has made my dream come true. I have been to more than eighteen nations but I have been through many trials and tribulations, five car accidents, and much more. There is much more to say and I'm still going strong to focus on my dream. My dream is to make other people's dreams come true. There are three essential ingredients that are working for me and help me to stay focused on my life's dream through the difficult times. Sometimes there are dangers and detours that come from many ways.

1. Compassion and passion in any dream, mission, or marriage can lose the passion you felt when you first said yes to it. But marriage, it is a choice to love your spouse unconditionally. When they don't smell good, when they don't feel good, when they don't look good. At the end of the month or in the middle of the month. It is a choice. You must choose to love because Christ chose to go to the cross. He didn't have to but he chose. Remember, life is not full of cherries or roses, or money in the bank with an unlimited account. So only compassion and passion can help you to fulfill God's dream. To love your wife or your neighbor is a choice. To give them freedom to come and go as they choose. To respond with positive feeling that led you down this path initially. Initiate romance even when you don't feel it. Somehow I confess that I was to busy doing ministry and that I neglected my marriage. I have learned much since the loss of my companion. Oh how I want to be happy. I wanted to repair, to encourage, my mate at the time but instead I was wounded deep in my soul. I could not reach my mate. Maybe this sounds like you, or you're going through something like it. Life is not fair, but God is good.

2. Patience and kindness is instant gratification but relationship, it is a lifetime achievement. It is not a one day service or an instant development. We have forgotten how to wait. This one word is used throughout the bible, wait on the Lord, trust and wait on God. We need FAITH, day after day, and moment after moment, to stay focused.
3. Providence and persistence and perseverance, these are the powerful keys to success in all living. Expect God's divine intervention. Look for it and recognize it when it happens. In times of deep frustration, when you cannot handle the pain or frustration of apparent failure, give God a chance to turn the obstacle into a new opportunity in your journey. I hope this will be beneficial to you.

Abraham Lincoln, history tells us, ran for president seventeen times and he lost every time. Not only that but he was in a mental hospital for two years. Then he became one of the most heroic heroes, presidents and founders of this great America. If he did it, you can too. Don't throw away your tomorrow but redeem it instead.

> Jeremiah 29:11-14 declares: For I know the thoughts that I think toward you, saith the Lord, thoughts of peace, and not of evil, to give you an expected end. Then shall ye call upon me, and ye shall go and pray unto me, and I will hearken unto you. And ye shall seek me, and find me, when ye shall search for me with all your heart. And I will be found of you, saith the Lord: and I will turn away your captivity, and I will gather you from all the nations, and from all the places whither I have driven you, saith the Lord; and I will bring you again into the place whence I caused you to be carried away captive.

I recall that for more than three years I went on serving the Lord without Angela. It seemed that the more that I fasted, the more that I prayed for her, the further away she drew from me and the ministry. Finally I asked the Lord why she was not coming back. I heard God's voice saying to me, "I give my people free will. I am not a dictator. I do not force anyone to confine to my word." The words of Jesus said, if you abide in me then I will abide in you. You ask me anything and I will do it but I will not force people to love out of my love. (See John 15:7) Then, I remembered that

> 1 Corinthians 7:15-16 declares, "But if the unbeliever leaves, let him leave. A brother and a sister are not bound by such occasions. For your wife, how do you know if you will save your husband, or your husband, how do you know if you will save your wife?"

HOW CAN I LET GO?

Here are a few comments about wisdom that I have achieved and gleaned from many mentors that God brought in my life.

1. To let go means I can't do it for someone else, but to not stop caring.
2. To let go is the realization that I can't control another, but not to cut myself off.
3. To let go is to allow learning from natural consequences, not to enable.
4. To let go means the outcome is not in my hands, that I admit powerlessness.
5. To let go means that I can only change myself, not to try to change or blame another.
6. To let go is to care about, not to care for.
7. To let go is to be supportive, not to fix.
8. To let it go is to allow another to be a human being, not to judge.
9. To let go is to allow another to affect their own outcomes, not to be in the middle arranging their outcome.
10. To let go is to permit another to face reality, not to be protective.
11. To let go is to accept, not to deny.
12. To let go is to search out my own shortcomings and correct them, not to nag, scold or argue with another.

13. To let go is to take each day as it comes and cherish the moment, not to adjust everything to my desires.
14. To let go is to try to become what I dream I can be, not to criticize or regulate anyone.
15. To let go is to live and grow for the future, not to regret the past.

And to let go is to love more and fear less! Finally, GOD says; "For GOD Has not given us a Spirit of fear, But one of power, Love and sound judgment."

If you have ever forgiven anyone for anything you are a hero. By the way, recently I received a phone call from Angelina and her husband Dick and I'm happy to hear that they are happy, and successful through their investments in real estate. I can truly say that God is a good God and a God of second chances.

PART 2

15
ITALY MISSION MIRACLE

Now it was September, 1993. It was almost time for the prophecy of God to be fulfilled concerning my trip to Italy which was given to me five years ago, by direct line from Christ. Unfortunately, I found myself in trouble. I didn't have a passport or the necessary document because all my important papers had been stolen from the mission home in Santa Ana. I tried to get a new document from the government and they informed me that they had no record of my existence in America because my file wasn't ever placed in the computer. After continuously trying Immigration told me that I would have to wait a minimum of nine months for them to search my file. I was very discouraged and disappointed because there was no way for me to go to Italy in 1993. But I knew that we serve a God that has unlimited resources and his word is true. What God says will always come to pass and the prophecy that God gave me in 1989 up in the mountain where I was fasting and praying was real and there was burning in my soul.

> Matthew 7:7 declares; "Ask and it shall be given unto you. Seek and you shall find, knock and it shall be opened unto you, for everyone who asketh, receiveth. All who seek, find, and everyone who knocks, it shall be open unto you".

Dr. Bruno Caporrimo

I prayed the prayer of faith and several days later something wonderful happened. I received a call from Chuck Hall, pastor of Trinity Broadcasting in Italy, inviting me to be the main speaker at T.B.N. They asked me to record the gospel in Italian for broadcasting to all of Italy and tell my testimony. I accepted. Several days later I met Paul Crouch, president of T.B.N., and Chuck Hall and his wife Nora. They expressed their gratitude and thanked me for bringing the gospel to the 61 million people in Italy. That night, as I went home after such a wonderful event and move of the Holy Spirit, I was full of joy and thanking and praising the Lord for allowing me to minister to the 61 million inhabitants of Italy through the television medium. I want to give thanks to Paul and Jan Crouch for being obedient to the vision that God has given them to build TV stations around the world, and also to Chuck Hall and his wife Nora for building many TV stations in Italy. They draw many to the Lord, so they too can have a honeymoon with the Holy Spirit. The Lord fulfilled the prophecy in my life even though I had no passport or transportation. God knew all along that it was possible to fulfill prophecy in someone's life in a way beyond their imagination or dreams.

I PRAYED AND ASKED THE LORD FOR A CHINESE WIFE

In December 1993, Pastor Mariano and I continued to minister together from the mission home. We also had a bilingual English-Chinese radio program to reach the Chinese in our local area. I found myself being very involved in the ministry but I had very little family life of my own. Then I began to make a petition to the Lord. I asked if it was okay for me to get married again, if it was his will to be accomplished in my life. After praying for thirty days and seeking the Lord, the power of the Holy Spirit filled the room and I heard God say to me, "Bruno, Bruno, what kind of wife do you want?" Well, I was startled. Now the God of the universe is asking me. I was trembling, speechless, I knew that quickly I had to give him an answer. I hesitated, I was startled, I opened my mouth and I shouted out, "Ch-ch-ch-ch-Chinese!!" In my soul I got up from my prayer closet. I knew that God was totally healing me from the scars of my past rejection. Of

Angelina's rejection and abandonment of me. Hallelujah!! I began to tell everybody. I began to preach it. I began to tell everybody that God was going to give me a Chinese wife. Mariano had introduced me to a spiritual mom, a Chinese lady. We will call her Mama Wong. She was a very special woman of God, full of character and a humble heart, and very successful in raising up family. One day I said to her, "Mama Wong, I too can have a Chinese wife." She replied, "Ah-hhh. I'll fix you up." Well, within two months she introduced me to ten Chinese ladies. Some played the piano, some were in full-time ministry, even some were very wealthy. One morning in prayer, I felt God rebuking me. He said to me, "You have asked me for a wife, why don't you wait until I bring her to you? Why are you opening your big mouth and looking in the wrong places?" He said, "Didn't I bring Eve to Adam?" There, in the presence of the Lord I began to repent and I said, "Father, please forgive me. Your ways are not my ways and your thoughts are not my thoughts."

Thirty days went by when, in my daily devotion one morning, the Lord opened my eyes. He gave me a vision of myself standing behind the pulpit and he showed me my bride to be. She was the most beautiful Chinese lady standing next to me. Then he showed me my ex-wife sitting in the pews among the sheep. I got so excited. I looked in the Spirit to my left and there she was, glowing and laughing. I said, "Lord, "Is she mine? She's beautiful!" God said, "Yes." I began praying aloud in my room, "Holy Spirit, bring me my spouse. Bring my maid to me," Continuously, day after day I would pray this. In the late part of that year a great Evangelist and mighty man of God, William Morris, invited me to share the word of God in his meeting. On Sunday night at 6 p.m., I walked into the church which was full of Chinese people. There was only one vacant chair at the back of the room. I went there and as I sat quietly in the chair. I looked to my right and there I saw this beautiful, attractive lady. My heart leaped and I said, "Lord, I would like to marry someone like that lady." Then I repented and said, "Lord, forgive me, I did not come here to look for a wife but to preach Your Word." After sharing my message, I passed out literature and asked people with a good voice to speak on the Christian radio. Then the MIRACLE came. Thirty days later the Lord sent Lydia to the mission home. She introduced herself to Pastor Mariano and his wife. She told them that someone by the name of Bruno gave her the flyer and that she was here to respond. That particular night I was not at home. I had been preaching and came home late and immediately had gone to bed. The next morning there was a knock on the door and Pastor Mariano's wife said to me, "Pastor Bruno, breakfast is ready." As I walked into the living room Lydia was standing there. I was startled and emotionally excited to see that she knew this family. The flyer had only indicated Pastor Mariano Yo and the radio program, she did not expect to find me there. She saw me and she was shocked. As we had breakfast and fellowship, the Holy Spirit told me that she would be my wife. While they were talking I got up and immediately ran into my room and got on my knees and prayed Matthew 6:6; But thou, when thou prayest, enter into the closet, and when thou hast shut the door, pray to the Father, which is in secret, and thy Father, which see in secret, shall reward thee openly.

I then asked the Lord for confirmation. If Lydia was to be my wife, that she would accompany me to the beach after the radio program to have some ice cream. That night after the radio program, as we were driving back to the mission home, I asked Lydia if she would like to go for a walk and have some ice cream. She accepted the invitation gladly. The incredible thing is that anyone who knows Lydia knows very well that Lydia goes to bed by 11 p.m. She becomes very sleepy and her eyes shut down and close automatically, like a Cinderella. But that night God was about to make a miracle by bringing China and Italy together. Bruno from Italy and Lydia from Taiwan, two different cultures, like vinegar and oil in a bottle, but when mixed together make the best Italian salad dressing. I believe that a good marriage is established through prayer. But, there are also trials and tribulations and the Lord was just beginning to confirm his word. He began to bind us together and confirm the blueprint for the ministry and the destiny that he had purposed for us. That night, as we began to walk on the beach under the full moon that shone upon us, I found myself walking and talking to Lydia and observing her. Her character and personality were so real and royal. My heart began to palpitate and I knew that the Lord had blessed me in sending Lydia into my life. As we continued to walk toward the pier, suddenly Lydia said to me, "Look, the moon is following us." I looked at my watch. It was midnight and the light of the silvery moon was guiding us. I felt so much joy and the presence of God was so real.

Suddenly I looked at Lydia and said, "It is time to pray". She responded, "Okay". As we looked deep into the moon hanging between the sky and the ocean, in all her fullness, we began to thank the Lord for His wonderful creation and stood together praying for all the nations. I rejoiced in my heart quietly and said, 'Thank you Lord," I was thankful that he brought me a prayer partner.

> Matt. 18:18-19: Verily I say unto you, "Whatsoever ye shall bind on earth shall be bound in heaven; and whatsoever ye shall loose on earth shall be loosed in Heaven. Again I say unto you, that if two of you shall agree on earth as touching anything that they shall ask, it shall be done for them of my father, which is in heaven."

I saw the miracle of the night, for the first time in my life. We both experienced something new. We watched the moon setting into the ocean so fast and so quickly that we both starred each other in the eyes and said, "Wow". I said to Lydia, "What does that mean?" She replied, "Your past and my past are now under the ocean, forever gone, and this is our new beginning." The following day, while having breakfast, Lydia mentioned that her father was ill in Taiwan and that she had to go there for awhile. I immediately went into my prayer closet. I began praying and I asked the Lord for another confirmation of Lydia being the perfect mate which he had ordained for me. I started to be impatient and confused. It seemed that she had just walked into my life and was now walking away. I remembered clearly praying to the Lord that I should be the one to take her to the airport. I prayed that she would accept my proposal and ring of engagement. I quoted the scripture:

> Mark11:23-24: For verily I say unto you, that whosoever shall say to this mountain, be thou removed and be cast into the sea and shall not doubt in his heart but shall believe that those things which he says shall come to pass, he shall have whatsoever things he sayeth. Therefore I say unto you that what things ever you desire when you pray, BELIVE, that you receive them and you shall have them.

As I worshipped the Father, the Son and the Holy Spirit, I went back to the kitchen area and Pastor Mariano asked me if I would take Lydia to the airport. I gladly accepted. It seemed to be the confirmation of what I had asked the Lord. That night, after arriving at Los Angeles airport and checking the baggage in, we still had two hours before the departure. I asked Lydia if she would like to have something to eat and she said, "Yes." We went to a 7-11 shop outside the airport. There was a group of people and Lydia and I began witnessing and passing out tracts to them. Some accepted the Lord in their hearts. I started rejoicing because I could see that Lydia had the same desire and burden for lost souls as I do. Then, as we headed back to the airport, I drove to the Hilton Hotel instead. She exclaimed, "What are we doing here?" I said, "Be calm, I want to show you something." As we walked through the lobby into a royal banquet room, I asked her to sit. I got on my knees before her and took out this very big ring and told her, "Lydia, you are going away for thirty days. I want you to be my special girl. But if you should find someone else, then return the ring back to me." She began to smile and said, "This ring is too big for me. Someone might try to steal it from me," She accepted it gladly. We returned to the airport and as I watched her leave, I felt sad and lonely. It was as though part of my being was leaving me since I was not going with her.

16
THE FUTURE MINISTRY - ASIA

That night, while going back to my mission home, I began to praise the Lord. I asked God to give me more confirmation concerning Lydia. I wanted confirmation for my life, our marriage and our ministry. The following day, I began to change my prayer life and focused more on Taiwan and China and prayed for Lydia and our family. I found myself visualizing what it would be like to be in China. I sensed a new anointing and freshness in my life, like I had not felt before. For the next thirty days I found myself speaking and praying with Lydia on the telephone. I found myself prophesying to her. I began to find myself in a controversial situation. She indicated she was unable to come back to the States, "I need to take care of my papa. He is scheduled for surgery and the doctors want to amputate his leg because of diabetes." I would begin to pray and prophesy to her, "Lydia, you need to come back to the States. We are going to college together. We are going to get married and serve the Lord together. We will go to China together." She would respond to me, "You're crazy. How can that be? I am not as anointed as you are. I do not know anything about the ministry."

For thirty days, I would spend an hour on the phone ministering to Lydia in prayer and prophesy because I was in love. After thirty days I had accumulated a 300 dollar phone bill. Lydia returned to the States. For the next 3 years, God opened up the door for me to pursue Lydia. She lived 70 miles away from my mission home. Through many trials, tribulations, and difficulties, I found out that after devotion, spending time with the Holy Spirit, and having a honeymoon with the Holy Spirit, He would guide my steps. "The steps of a good man are ordered by the Lord and he delights in his ways." (Psalm 37:23.) Day after day, I found myself driving to Lydia's home and making plans. I was going to meetings and Bible studies. The Lord began moving us to minister to many Chinese people. My plan was to marry Lydia as soon as possible. I was anxious to get started in our ministry. I was confident about the prophetic word that I had received from the Lord that Lydia was my wife and we were going to have a ministry together. Week after week, our friendship grew but when I would mention marriage she would say to me, "I like your anointing. I like to minister with you. But I do not want to marry you." I would find myself driving back to Orange County. To my mission home, 70 miles, discouraged and talking to the Lord. I said, "Lord you have made a mistake. She does not want to marry me." I thought, "Maybe, Lord, I should never get married. Just keep my honeymoon with you, serve you and never be married." I closeted myself for three days, seeking the Lord and worshipping and praising Him. During those three days, the Lord filled me with His love and a strong burden for me to continue pursuing Lydia. I found myself driving to where she worked. Right next to where she worked there was a supermarket. I went in, bought two-dozen roses, and asked the delivery boy to deliver the flowers to her. I instructed him to ask her if she would take the flowers and have dinner with me. I positioned myself behind a telephone pole where I could see her through the window receiving the flowers. I watched her expression light up. I know that the Lord had directed my steps because Lydia loves flowers. Immediately, the boy came back and said to me, "Okay, she will go out with you."

That night at dinner, we found ourselves walking on the hillside of a mountain and praying for three hours for the nations of the world. After three months I noticed how much Lydia loved the Lord. She would go to Bible studies, meetings, conferences and the more I watched her loving the Lord, the more I knew in my heart that the Lord was doing something special in our lives. Once again I proposed to Lydia. She responded that 9 out of 10 friends old her not to marry me because I was Italian and too radical and wild for the Lord. She also responded she would never marry me because I did not have a doctorate degree.

From Mafia Boss to the Cross

She said, "Get one and I will marry you." I told her that this was crazy. I felt that I did not qualify to be a scholar and earn a degree. God had a different plan. Hallelujah!! One day while Lydia was sharing with my students at the Bible Training Center, she challenged the students to set up five goals that they wanted God to answer in their life. I found myself writing five goals:

1. I want to marry Lydia.
2. I want to get my Doctorate degree.
3. I want to go to Taiwan.
4. I want a building for the Bible School and Training Center.
5. I want a better running car.

I wrote this down in my Bible and everyday I prayed out loud. My prayer was like this:

"Thank you Lord that I am going to marry Lydia, thank you Lord for my new car, thank you Lord for the building, and thank you Lord that I am going to Taiwan. Thank you Lord for leading me to the right Bible College to get my doctorate degree."

The scripture that I stood firm was Mark 11:23-24: Verily I say unto you, that whosoever shall say to this mountain, be thou removed and be thou cast unto the sea; and shall not doubt in his heart, but shall believe that those things which he saith shall come to pass, he shall have whatsoever he saith.

BIBLE COLLEGE

Wonderful reader, the greatest thing is that God is so faithful. Within three days God began to manifest His hand and the miracle began for me to enter Bible College. To give you all the details as to how this came about, I would have to write another book. I am hoping that you can read between the lines and visualize how God moved. Especially when you build yourself in HIS romantic, loving way and have a honeymoon with the Holy Spirit!! I was not the only one that joined the Bible College. Lydia joined with me also.

THE BUILDING

Several weeks had gone by when one of the students shared with me that there was a building available. Within thirty days we got the building. It is the building we have today in Anaheim.

THE CAR

Shortly after, we were planning an outreach to Las Vegas. Three days before leaving, my mechanic warned me not to go with my old van. He said that it was too old and would never make it over the mountains and desert. My only response was, "I have to go. We are scheduled to go tonight. What am I going to do?" My mechanic responded, "Take this car that I am selling and use it for your outreach." As soon as I got in the car the Holy Spirit spoke to me, "This is your car." As we drove to Las Vegas, we worshipped and shared the Lord all the way up there. The hand of the Lord was upon us. In three days in Las Vegas, we saw about 160 people saved in the casinos and outside the parking lot. I watched the Lord anoint Lydia and transform her with the personality God had given her. People were responding to us. When we returned home, our friend the mechanic was in the hospital. His wife informed me that he had a heart problem. The following day I went to the hospital to visit him. I knelt at the foot of his bed in his hospital room and began to pray with him. I asked the Lord for divine healing. Three days later he was dismissed from the hospital with a new heart. I rejoiced as he went back to work. He thanked me for praying for him. He said, "The least I can do is give you the car and the title." Thank you JESUS!!

During the next three years I lived as a full-time minister and attended Bible School. The Bible College required a thesis and a dissertation to get a Doctorate degree. Dr. Alexander, the Founder of Living Word Bible College, asked me to teach prophecy at the Bible School to pastors and Laymen. I found myself very busy. Yet I was never too busy to stop the desire of marrying Lydia and filling the void in my life according to God's prophecy. Again I proposed to Lydia. Again she rejected me. With much disappointment, I decided to break away from Lydia. For four to five days I did not contact her at all. In my view this relationship was one-sided. I was the aggressor and I was tired of rejection. I came to a conclusion. I would end the relationship.

A few days later she left me a message and invited me to minister with her to some of her Chinese friends. I decided to call her back and leave a message. Very calmly I explained that it was not right for the relationship to continue, since she did not want to marry me. I said that it was better to separate so the Lord could work in her life to give her the man of her dreams.

LYDIA'S STORY (FOURTH GOAL)

When I received the message from Bruno I knew the relationship had ended. That same day one of my spiritual mothers called me. She asked for Bruno. She said that a Chinese pastor wanted to meet him and for him to minister in China. For the sake of the ministry, I humbled myself and paged Bruno three times with no response. That evening I felt something was missing. I felt lost. I checked my heart and realized that I really liked Bruno. All night long I was not able to sleep. Early in the morning the Holy Spirit prompted me to kneel down. If Bruno was mine he would come back. Later, in my devotion I looked out on the balcony where there was a tall tree with large branches. Two baby doves were on the branch. Suddenly one flew away and the other remained on the stem alone, cold and shivering.

The Holy Spirit revealed to me that this was my situation. Before noon time, my elderly spiritual mother asked me to come over for lunch and have fellowship. She mentioned Bruno. She said that he was anointed, had a healing gift, boldness, and would preach repentance without compromise. She said that we, the Chinese people, needed someone like him. She mentioned about wanting to serve the Lord and that it was not good to be alone. I felt the Lord's gentle words speaking to me through my spiritual mom and the confirmation of the dove birds of earlier that morning. I really searched my heart and I knew I longed for Bruno. The special feelings for Bruno were very real and strong in my life. I confess to you, I repented and realized I had taken my relationship with Bruno for granted for the past three years. At this moment, the conviction of God was on me and for the first time. I knew Bruno was God's gift sent to me, to fulfill God's plan and destiny in my life. I knew the ministry was to bring God's glory. Miraculously, Bruno came back that evening and we went to the pastor's home to fellowship and pray. We received the blessing to get the marriage license and be married. That night the Holy Spirit honeymoon experience became real to Lydia. Within two months we were married, on October 21, 1995. We were married in the Bible College. The marriage ceremony was heaven on earth with different races, yellow, black and white. Over 250 people attended. We entered together into the Honeymoon with the Holy Spirit. Our marriage is truly the work of the Lord. I could write a book just on all the trials and tribulations and blessings we have received. He gives many blessings when, in faithfulness, we truly submit to the Holy Spirit. When we love Him with all our mind, soul, and strength. This is not easy. It requires process, and day after day, seeking Him. Then, and only then, transformation comes. To live each day in the victorious life that a marriage can possess. Life is not fair, but God is good.

By the way, at this very moment while Dominic and I are finishing this chapter, OUR FAITH WAS BEING TESTED ONCE AGAIN! We received a knock at the door by a homeless lady. She is in her fifties or maybe early sixties. She told us to call 911 because she was in much pain. Her legs and her body were full of pain. We responded, "Let's pray for you and if it does not work, if you are not better, then we will call 911." We began to pray and within 5 minutes the power of God came down. She fell down and began to shake. We began to sing songs to the Lord. We told her, "Do you feel better?" She replied, "No, I have a terrible headache!" Then she insisted that I call 911. I hesitated. I was going to call 911, then I remembered James 5:13-14, which declares: "If anyone among you is sick, call the elders of the church and anoint them with oil. And the prayer of faith will make the sick well."

I told my assistant, "Run to the church and get the oil." Dominic ran to the church sanctuary and came back with a big bottle of olive oil. I put the oil over her head and prayed the prayer of faith. We sang one song and then we walked away. We continued writing the book. Three minutes later I went to check on the lady and I was told that she walked away well. Praise God, for another miracle in this chapter!! By the way, if we were to call 911 we would have the ambulance, the firemen, the police, and a big bill to pay. But we remembered that God says, "When you are sick, call upon me, I am the Lord thy God that healeth thee." (Exodus 15:26) Who do you call when there is trauma in somebody's life? If we learn and remember the glory and the power of God then we could eliminate a lot of chaos. You must say, but Brother Bruno, "Will God answer me?" Why don't you try when your life is turmoil and everything goes wrong. Let God be the 911. He will turn things around and give you the crown!!

17
TAKING ON THE WORLD FOR THE MASTER

In early December, a few months after we were married, we planned to go to Taiwan to visit my new family. A few days before the flight we went to Hacienda Heights to visit Joseph and Serene. They were both of Chinese descent, from Taiwan. These two really loved the Lord. As we arrived at their home, Joseph inspired us to go and preach at his church in Taiwan called 'The Good News Church'. We accepted the invitation gladly and with great expectations. We had much joy in our heart and were excited to see what God was going to do. Flyers were made and I was scheduled to preach for three days.

We arrived in Taiwan and were greeted by my new family. We were informed papa, Lydia's father, was in the hospital. In 24 hours they were going to amputate his leg due to diabetes. We rushed to the hospital where I encountered this wonderful man. He received me gladly. Within 15 minutes we lead him into the sinner's prayer and he accepted Christ. I watched Lydia's expression. She was rejoicing and full of Joy. Within a few seconds her uncle walked in and also accepted Christ. As I sat him in the chair, he experienced the electricity and the power of the Holy Spirit pass through him. He shouted, "I feel God, I feel God!!" A few minutes later, the intern warden and the doctors walked in and informed us that they were going to amputate papa's legs. Immediately I plead with papa and said, "Please don't do it! Cancel the surgery for three days." Papa asked, "Why? My legs are swollen like a potato and I don't have any circulation." Once again I plead with him to postpone the surgery for three days.

Through my agony I tried to explain that God was going to heal him. "Papa you have nothing to lose. They are going to cut off the legs anyway. Why not give me three days?" He sat there thinking then responded, "Okay, I will speak to the doctors and postpone the surgery for three days." My wife and I rejoiced as we waited for about 45 minutes so papa could give the doctors the announcement. The surgeon came rushing through the door. He looked at me in the eyes and exclaimed, "You are an American, we are doctors, why are you causing this delay? We are scheduled to amputate the legs tomorrow at 2:00!" However, God was moving and Papa had made his decision. Lydia and I vowed to fast and pray for the next three days. Dear reader, I hope you are catching on to what we are up to. You have already read part of my life story, that I had spent three days a week fasting and praying on the mountain for five years. For 72 hours we began to seek, fast and pray for Papa. We only drank water. On the third day Lydia and I walked in the hospital. As I kneeled at Papa's hospital bed and anointed him with oil, the Holy Spirit jumped on Papa and healed his legs. Dear reader, there was a tremendous power released into this wonderful man. Within a couple of hours, x-rays were taken and showed that the circulation had been restored in his legs. The doctors saw the miracle through the x-rays. They saw where the legs were restored. Hallelujah! Papa stayed in the hospital for a few more days.

> Psalms103:1-3: Bless the Lord, O my soul, and all that is within me, bless his Holy name. Bless the Lord, O my soul, and forget not all his benefits. Who forgiveth all thine iniquities; who healeth all thy diseases.

As we continued in total submission to the Holy Spirit, the Lord began to move through our lives. We are grateful to be able to share this with you. We began the three day crusade in 'The Good News Church'. I watched 200 people worshipping the Lord in Chinese. I asked the Lord, "Lord what would you like to teach here tonight?" The Lord said to teach prophecy and prophesy to all of them. Dear reader, I ministered until 1 a.m. with a great interpreter named Julie. I found out the people who were being prophesied to would get back in line for more. Finally Lydia began to shout it is late, that we have to stop, and that people were sneaking back in line. We finally closed down the meeting. The next day, at a moments notice, the Lord led us to have a Chinese wedding. Pastor Ko, the senior pastor, Pastor Amy, and part of the congregation helped us to have a wonderful wedding in the hospital where Papa was staying. Pastor Ko and Pastor Amy performed the ceremony. The next day Papa was released from the hospital. Once again, I want to express my gratitude to the Good News Church for giving us a supernatural wedding. For giving us a wedding of heaven on earth. The very next day, Julie our interpreter and crusade administrator, arranged several meetings with a very well known minister in Asia and other parts of the world. His name was Pastor Tai. We found out later that he was the founder of a very large prayer mountain years ago. He had engaged all the churches in Taiwan for prayer and revival. After we met him and his wife, he requested me to prophesy for all his co-workers. There were more than fifty of them. The service began at 2 p.m. with praise and worship. Working with Julie as my translator, the Holy Spirit began to come down in a tremendous and incredible move of God. The prophetic gifts were manifesting through us and within three to four hours we managed to prophesy to everyone.

I remember as I began to walk towards the office to get away from the crowd, a young woman grabbed my arm. She said, "Pastor Bruno, you did not pray for me. I am the pastor's niece." As I looked into her eyes, I saw such a love and compassion. Radiant beauty was flowing through her. She was so sweet and so kind. I could not find it in my heart to say no to the words that came out of her mouth. I replied, "Please come to your uncle's office and have some tea with us. I will prophesy to you." Shortly after while we were drinking tea in the office with Pastor Tai, his sister and other family members including his niece, joined us. The niece kept insisting and demanding a prophecy from the Lord. I began to pray. I requested this prophecy be taped. I have learned through experience that after prophesying people get emotional and start to cry. Shortly after, they forget the prophecy. Many times people call me and ask me, "Pastor Bruno do you remember what God said about me?" Obviously, as I travel around the nations using the gift of prophecy, I am not able to remember every prophesy that I give. I have a custom to tape the prophecies that are given out.

Dear reader, thank God we had a tape that day. What I am going to share with you has touched many people and will touch you also. While we were praying the prophetic anointing started to activate in my mouth for her. I said, "Frances, I see the Lord is going to take you to England, to obtain your Master degree. You will be there several years. I see this very big college, a very large building and there is a bridge to go to this college. You are going to meet a man at this school. He is not Chinese, he is an Englishman and this man is sent from God to you. He will help you and you are going to marry him. The Holy Spirit shows me the size of this man not the face. He is about 5'11" to 6 feet tall and he is thirty years old. He has dark hair. You will come back to Taiwan and he will come back with you." After the prophecy was over, the room became very quiet. I come to find out the mother was a very traditional Chinese woman and would never allow any of her children to marry outside the Chinese culture. We finished the three day meeting with Pastor Tai.

This was in 1995. Since then our ministry has been to Taiwan more than 35 times. It has expanded to all the island of Taiwan. Something wonderful happened in 1999, which I am about to share with you.

We received a phone call in Taiwan from Frances. She shared with us that the prophecy came to pass. She wanted to meet with us so that we could meet her fiancee. Several hours later we met. She shared with us every detail of how the Lord put her and her fiancee together. They were planning the wedding in the next few months. She also shared that she was glad that the prophecy was on tape for her parents to hear. Had the prophecy not been on tape, her parents would not have allowed the wedding. She also shared that all the women in her wedding wanted a prophecy so that they too could marry a white man. We rejoiced for Frances. God brought a wonderful man into her life and the Holy Spirit worked out every detail to bring to pass the prophecy. I believe that God will continue to do much more for both of them as they continue a honeymoon together with the Holy Spirit.

Revelation 19:10
And I fell at his feet to worship him. And he said unto me, See thou do it not: I am thy fellow servant, and of thy bretheren that have the testimony of Jesus: worship God: for the testimony of Jesus is the spirit of prophesy.

Dr. Bruno Caporrimo

In 1996 The Good News Church scheduled us for a 30 day conference in equipping and teaching on how to win souls. The conference was located in the city of Taipei, Taiwan. We gladly accepted. After the conference was over, a precious lady named Susan Yan approached us. She is an architect and anointed minister of the gospel. She was very well known and respected in her community. She asked my wife and I if we would go to a local hospital to minister to, Huang Shao Tung, a lady friend of hers. I found out that she was a very famous singer. Of course we agreed to do so and arrived at the hospital the following day. After suffering a stroke, Susan's friend was severely incapacitated. She was paralyzed on the entire right side of her body, including her face. Her speech was impaired and slurred and her hands were curled into a gnarled claw shape. I immediately withdrew to a corner to pray. I asked the Lord directly and simply, "Lord, what caused this?" The Lord spoke to me very clearly and said, "Rebuke the curses off of her."

Suddenly the glory of God was manifested in the room. The anointing of the Holy Spirit was evident in a very dynamic way. I could see with my spiritual eyes that a demonic oppression was leaving her. The Holy Spirit told me quite plainly that seven spirits were to come out of her and that I must command healing to enter her body. I was overwhelmed by the excitement of the moment. I told my wife Lydia that God was going to heal this woman. Anointing her with oil, I commanded healing for her bent spine and the chemical imbalance in her body. At that moment, before our eyes, her twisted hand, arm and shoulder began to miraculously straighten and be restored to a normal, healthy state. Hallelujah! Her husband was on his knees with his face buried in the bed. He was weeping aloud and pleading with God for her deliverance. I shouted to him, "Look! Look!" As he looked up at his beloved wife, his agony turned to tearful joy and praise. The woman had totally recovered after only ten minutes of prayer and supplication. The Lord had worked a mighty miracle! I returned to the corner of the room and began to thank and praise the Lord. Her husband tapped me on the shoulder and told me: "I have a bad kidney and a terrible pain in my back." After I anointed him with oil and prayed over him, he fell to the floor. As I continued to pray over him, the door suddenly burst open and several doctors, nurses and even the Director of the hospital marched in. They were very upset and demanded to know what I was doing to their patients. The scene was absolute bedlam.

The lady was shouting "Hallelujah." Her husband appeared to be dead on the floor and my wife and I were loudly praising the Lord. Can you imagine how this appeared to these non-believers? I explained to them that we were pastors and then we quickly left the hospital. Susan's friend was released from the hospital within three days in perfect health. A few months later, we conducted a Friday Night Healing Service at the Good News Church in Taipei. Susan's friend and her husband shared their first hand testimony of this mighty miracle. They also touched our lives with their anointed ministry of Gospel songs and books they had written. Presently, this wonderful couple serves the Lord full time with a music ministry that is well known in Asia and around the world.

They also share this creative miracle that God gave them. Everywhere that I go, whether it's New York City or California, there's always someone that recognizes me. They say, "I know who you are. You're that Bruno guy who prayed for the famous Chinese singer." I have come to the conclusion that God knows what he's doing. God knows who's faithful. He acknowledged this humble couple. They are in their late fifties and they travel all over and continue to broadcast the Good News!! You might say, well it's easy for them. Well, it's not so easy. They have their ups and downs, lows and highs. But they continue steadfast and the follow the journey and the dream that God has layed before them. What about you? Are you willing to take time and seek God's plan for your life? I assure you that he will not fail you when everything comes against you. When life is not fair, remember, God is good! He will pick you up, put you together and give you hope.

18
HEAVENLY CROWN ON HIS HEAD

In 1996 the roof caved in. I remember it was about 5 p.m. when my sister-in-law called us from Taiwan and I heard struggling words coming out from her mouth. She said, "Bruno, Papa passed away. He went with Jesus." I was shocked and speechless. There on my right is my bride asking me, "What is she saying, what is she saying?" I held her arm and said, "Lydia, we need to go to Taiwan right away because p-p-p-p-papa passed away. He's with Jesus." We felt the roof cave in. My wife, she fell on the floor crying. I began to cry. We cried our eyes out for over an hour. The elders and the people from my church came to my home. They began to pray for us and encourage us. We were broken-hearted and emotionally stressed out because we did not expect that this tragedy would hit us so soon. It had only been six months since the Lord Jesus healed his legs and he came home healthy. My spirit was disturbed. I knew there had to be some answers to all the questions I had in my mind. Over fifty members of the church began to pray for both of us. God opened my eyes. In the Holy Spirit I saw my father –in- law in heaven with a crown on his head smiling and looking great. I said, "Lord was is that?" The Lord, more specifically the inner voice of the Holy Spirit said to me, "Bruno stop crying. Papa's in heaven with me. Get up and make preparations to go to Taiwan. I have a work for you to do!"

From Mafia Boss to the Cross

Wow, God always answers the prayers of his children. DISAPPOINTED, YOU BET. DISCOURAGED, VERY MUCH. DEFEATED, NOT ANY MORE!! I turned to my bride and I shared my vision and my little Chinese bride suddenly smiled. Everybody smiled. Boldness came over us and our strength was restored. We reorganized a strategy, a plan, and the following day we went on a new mission. That night the Holy Spirit showed me a very large bulletin program. It was written all in Chinese and in the very middle, in large print it said; 'PASTOR BRUNO CAPORRIMO.' Well, a month and a half later there was the family bulletin. You see, my father-in-law he was a very honored dignitary and very well respected in his community. The people that attended the wake were more than a thousand. To my surprise, when I arrived in Taiwan, we found that the family had redeemed the body of Papa and put him in the Buddah temple. For two weeks the Monks would come over to the house and chant a ritual ceremony more than two hours each day. I found this new to me and disgusting. It was the tradition of idol worshipping. I began to plea with my brother-in-law and my sister-in-law saying, "No, no, no, papa is in heaven. He's a Christian. You need not to do this. You need to give him a Christian wake." They responded to me, "We don't know a Christian service, furthermore, Papa wasn't water baptized."

Well, I knew they were ignorant of the things of God. THERE I opened up the Bible and every time I had the opportunity I was explaining things to them. I was explaining to them Scriptures. Three weeks went by when my wife's bigger brother Jimmy began to listen to me very carefully. He explained to me that I happened to be right but that the custom was to follow that religion. When we investigated why Papa died so soon, we were told that he drank some poisoned water.

I remember watching these Buddha people coming over and chanting for more than three weeks. They charged the family more than 50,000 dollars. Unfortunately the majority of the people in Taiwan don't have that kind of money for donations. They get a fast burial. The time came for the funeral and my brother-in-laws wife, who was a deaconess in the Buddha temple where the funeral was to be attended, had a plan. They were going to have the wake there, where people could come and give their last good-byes. She came into our house early in the morning and with a very friendly attitude she gave me these temple shoes and said,

Dr. Bruno Caporrimo

"These are for the funeral service, put them on." Out of ignorance of the Scriptures I put them on and suddenly I had pain in my feet. A few minutes later she said goodbye and walked out of the room. I saw a large dragon going by the room, just like it was a pet. Maybe you are like me, you've never been to a Buddha funeral. I learned to trust God. By faith my curiosity was building up and I was looking forward to seeing how they conducted this Chinese funeral. I have watched many movies about the Orient but now it was real. I remember that it was about 11 a.m. and someone brought the program schedule. When I opened it up I saw Chinese writing in oil paintings. It was very attractive. In the middle it said; PASTOR BRUNO CAPORRIMO. I was told that I was to do something in the funeral. I remembered that this was a confirmation that God was in control. This was confirmation of the vision that God gave me and I had peace. At 1:00 p.m. we arrived at the funeral parlor. There were over 60 women who very well dressed in blue and white. They were chanting to Buddha. The conference room held more than 1,000 people. It was packed to the wall. I watched the master of ceremony conducting the service in a way that I never saw before in any other funeral service that I have attended. This seemed very traditional and it was strange. Believe it or not the Holy Spirit opened my eyes and I could see the spiritual warfare. There were demons flying all over the place. I felt like they were saying to me, "Hey you're a Christian. You are in the wrong place!" But somehow within me, the power of God was building up in me. It was so strong that I wish I could have choked those demons and killed them with my own hands. I was saying to myself, HOW DARE YOU DECEIVE THESE WONDERFUL, BEAUTIFUL PEOPLE.

The master of ceremony would get a group, a family, and direct them to give condolences to the immediate family. They had a large painting of the 'Queen of Heaven' on the wall above. The rule was for each individual to bow three times and give reverence. Then they would turn to the right and bow to the picture on the wall of the deceased member. Two hours later they called my name. After my name was acknowledged, my bride and I, were supposed to follow the ritual service and kneel down. I remember that we discussed prior to that, that we would not kneel down to any idols. So we were ready to stand for our faith. You might say, "Well Brother Bruno, what's the difference whether you kneeled down or not?" The difference is the Ten Commandments. Exodus 20:4 says, "I am the Lord your God. I am a jealous God and you shall not bow down to any idols which are in heaven or below the earth."

God made these rules. We were not about to offend anybody, the family or their religion, but now we were on the spot. If we were to kneel down the family would be very happy. If we resist this temptation then we win! What I mean by that is to obey the laws of God. Under such pressure I said a little prayer to the Lord, "Lord, help me to be nice so nobody would get hurt." I remember saying a few things to the family and saying, "We rejoice that Papa is not on the wall anymore. He is in heaven which is a better place." The conductor is commanding us to kneel down. As I said, before this we had already discussed that we would not bow down to anymore idols. Hell broke loose. We watched a thousand people's faces change, including Lydia's family. They were loveable, sweet, forgiving, and the kindest people on the earth. Now I see hate manifesting in their lives towards us and another character in them was manifesting, before our very eyes. I could feel that they wanted to kill us. We felt like Shadrach, Mesach, and Ebendigo. Several minutes went by and they caught on that I was an Italian-American. That I would not submit to their tradition. As we stood firm they marveled and overlooked it. So the pressure was off for a-while.

A few minutes later they took the body into a different area that had a very large furnace where they would burn the deceased to be cremated. They proceeded to burn it in front of all of us. Prior to this I saw the family pushing and encouraging the children to put money in the coffin. By doing so, that was to bring them many blessings later according to their tradition and religion which was Buddhism. Then they proceeded with the ritual ceremony and dropped the body in the furnace to burn it. As I watched this unfold before my very eyes I was exhausted and frustrated to see this frustrating ritual taking place. But yet, to them, it is there way of life. Because they served the god of this world not the God of the bible. A while later, as we went to the house, the family got together and they began to rebuke and hit my wife over and over. They told her that she brought a curse to the traditional funeral and offended the ancestors. Now that I look back, these people needed the Lord and we as Christians, we have a lot to learn about life.

In that moment I responded, "In the name of Jesus, Satan I rebuke you, get out of here." I knew that I was caught up in spiritual warfare. I suddenly grabbed my wife and ran out of that house and went to a local church and got prayer. Because we were spiritually under pressure, we needed to be revived. The very next day we went back home. All the elders of the family said to us, "We need a man like Bruno to build a church in Taiwan and we will help them." Wow, I was shocked. You know and I know that it was God moving in. We had been faithful to believe what the Bible says. In Romans 8:28 it says that "We know that all things work for the good for those that love the Lord." Now, I can easily say that Taiwan needs many missionaries like me because it is the number one idol worshipper in the world. We know we cannot change anyone but I can truly say, in all honesty, from the bottom of my heart that we have so much peace to know that my father-in-law is in heaven. The Bible is very clear. In Romans 10:9-10 it says, if you confess with your mouth and believe in your heart that God raised Christ from the dead you shall be saved. Well, I'm a witness that my father-in-law made peace with God. Whether anyone believes us or not, is their choice. My father-in-law was a very righteous man. Maybe, yes, he worshipped idols because that's all he knew but later he believed in Christ. That settles it!! I will see him again. When Jesus Christ comes back to take the church home. What about you?? Are you willing to believe the Good Book? Jesus is willing to take you in. Don't miss this opportunity. LET HIM IN BECAUSE IT IS THE ONLY NORMAL THING TO DO. HE HAS A PLAN AND PURPOSE AND DESTINY FOR YOUR LIFE'S JOURNEY.

In 1997 I continued the training center in our home in Anaheim, California. Day after day, and week after week, I drove the long distance to Pomona Bible College where we attended. Dr. Alexander was pressuring me to complete the dissertation for my Doctorate degree. I continued to work hard and studied four to five hours a day. Finally, at the end of 1997, my graduation from Bible College was approaching. After reviewing my dissertation, they accepted it. This was my first book entitled, "Snake In the Glass". Already this book has been printed in four languages. The Bible College that I attended had over 600 members. They were all praying for us, for Taiwan, and for China. We are grateful to Dr. Alexander and the Living Word Bible College for always praying for us. I felt God had given me a heavy burden to reach and to train the Asian people.

When we choose to have a Honeymoon with Him, He helps us to obey His laws. The word Law means to "point the way". When people are born, as babies, they are raised on LOVE and not on the LAW. The law comes later. God put the LAW first in the old covenant so that we might understand the how and why of LOVE is supremely better than the law. The reason is simple. The LAW doesn't work. LOVE does!! The LAW separates, LOVE joins. The LAW divides, LOVE unites. The LAW is feared. LOVE rears. Love begins and never ends. It just gets better and better. The law merely stops the foolish man cold in his tracks, giving him an opportunity to look back and ahead. Another time to consider which way to go. Heaven above or hell below. The law was written for foolish men, to establish boundaries for them. But LOVE has no boundaries or limits! When we truly fall in love with God above, there are no more limits, restrictions or boundaries needed. That is why the Bible says that, as new covenanters, God has taken away all of our fears and wiped away all of our tears. Because we are no longer under the law but under Grace. GRACE is part and parcel of God's great love. It redeems us from the corpse of the LAW. LOVE lifts us so high that we can meet and come to know the Guy in the sky. In fact it's so high that we can never even come close to the LAW again because, in his GRACE, we have finally found what turned the world upside down-- that great, eternal, everlasting LOVESHIP! God says, "Invite me in and I will never leave you nor forsake you!" Can't we see that God intended for he and man to be forever married and bathed in grace. (Grace is short for "God's RACE" of people.)

With God's GRACE, the Ten Commandments of the Old Testament are GONE! Have the Ten Commandments ceased to exist? Heavens no! Where are they? The Ten have been swallowed up in the Two of the New Testament. The Two of the New are the LOVE commandments. The first is to LOVE God: the second is to LOVE your neighbor as yourself, for the LOVE of God! Jesus Christ yielded up his precious life as both God and man so that each of us could be given a choice, for ourselves, between Good and Evil. Just like our parents Adam and Eve had. But, as Jackie Gleason used to say to his TV wife, "Alice, you're the greatest". God surely is the greatest. He's the biggest LOVER of all time. I'd like to hug Him, but my arms are to short! Thank God that his arms are so long that they can reach around us all! God doesn't leave anything to chance. He's God and there is no one else like Him. Remember, God has chosen you and me to be ministers and priests of the Gospel OF Jesus Christ. God doesn't leave anything to chance. Let's read:

Rev. 1:5-6
And from Jesus Christ, who is the faithful witnesss, and the first, begotten of the dead, and prince of the Kings of the earth. Unto him that loved us, washed us from our sins in his own blood. And hath made us Kings and priests unto God and his Father to him be glory and dominion forever and ever, Amen.

REMEMBER, many a time God has reached out and called the ones who fall. Many have fallen, who God has called. What is the secret? What did Enoch, Noah, Abraham, Moses, Joshua, King David, King Solomon, Samson, Isaiah, Daniel, King Josiah, Paul, and all the many others have that we lack today? With few exceptions, they were all big sinners! Moses, David and Paul were admitted murderers. Noah got big time drunk at least once. Abraham, Moses, David, Solomon and Samson all had many women and multiple wives. What is the key to God's heart? Is LOVE the key to the secret victory? If that's the case, what does it take for us to fall in love with the man above?? How many books do you have to read before falling in love with someone? How much of the Bible do you have to read before you fall in LOVE with God? The word Bible spelled backwards is "El Bib" or God's book". God cannot be separated from His Word, the Bible. God says that HIS word will never change or end. (Everlasting Ministry wishes to give heart-felt thanks to Dr. Ben and Sally Lofstedt, and his family for all their support encouragement.)

19
UPCOMING MAYOR OF TAIPEI

In the year 2000 we received some other invitations to Taiwan and we were excited because our publisher was promoting my second book. After two months we had both small meetings and large meetings. We conducted seminars, we trained the local churches in spiritual warfare and equipped them in Evangelism. We also took the students, for several days, out to evangelize from home to home. One afternoon, there was a political rally going on for an election for the new mayor in Taipei, Taiwan. There were flags, music, a rally, and people shouting all over the place. There was so much excitement in the air. Some of the people approached us in very friendly conversation. They invited us to a reception celebration that was about to take place that afternoon. We accepted and before I knew it they escorted us in to the Government building. It was like the White House here in the United States. They knew that I was American. The Taiwanese people have a very great respect for the American people and for foreigners.

They escorted us into the front seat and gave us V.I.P. treatment. Suddenly the upcoming candidate walked towards me and smiled and shook my hand. He said, "I just came back from the States. I graduated from Harvard University and I'm running for political office in Taiwan." I was shocked. My response to him was, "I am here from America to support you." I don't even know why I said that. I was shocked because I'm a Minister. What do I know about politicians? I kept on saying to myself, "Why did I say this to him?" I looked at the crowd who welcomed and applauded this man. There was something special about this person, about his character, his personality. I watched him being introduced to the people. The crowd applauded him and then shouted. Well, fifteen or twenty minutes went by and he left. The flags and the banners were flying all over the air. People in Taiwan, when they elect someone, spend billions of dollars to elect their leaders. They invited us the following day and they asked Lydia if I would give a speech for fifteen minutes. I accepted. The next day we arrived at one in the afternoon and again they escorted us to the front. They sat me next to Ma Ying-Jeou's mother. She looked at me and said, "My son is a good boy. He never got in trouble when he was a kid. I pray that God is going to make him a mayor!"

As we watched the program unfolding I learned that many of them were Christian pastors. Others were not. At about three o'clock they called my name. It was my turn to share fifteen minutes. I opened my Bible and I shared with them that Romans 13 declares that it is God that gives you government leaders. Not only that, but that God would send his angel and give you the mayor. Many people shouted and applauded. Others in the crowd said, "Who do you think you are. We don't like this man, Ma Ying-Jeou." A few minutes later they were having a dinner reception. Something unusual was happening to me. I felt the small voice of God inside of me saying to me, "Go and pray." I did. I went to another room which was very dark and I kneeled down and began to pray intercession prayer for these lost souls. When I began praying, I heard in my spirit God saying to me, "Go and prophesy to Ma Ying-Jeou and tell him not to be discouraged. I will make him a mayor!" That night and the next day those words were ringing in my mind. I went to read my Bible. My favorite place to read was on top of the roof in my mother's house. I began my routine of devotional prayer and reading the Bible for more than three hours. I felt the unction of the Holy Spirit take over every area of my body and I knew that I was in the Spirit! I sent a telegram, in prayer, to the Lord. "Lord, I am afraid to go tell Ma Ying-Jeou that he is going to become a mayor. What if he doesn't become a mayor? My ministry in Taiwan would be destroyed and I would be a false prophet. Please Lord, give me a confirmation. Give me a sign!"

No sooner did I say that prayer, when my mind exploded in a zoom lens. I saw the Lord coming down and the area was filled with his Glory. By the way, I don't claim to be Moses or anyone special. I know that God uses the foolish to confound the wise. But there I am, standing in the Spirit, when I see the image and the face of the Lord Jesus Christ. Very firmly he spoke to me and out loud. With authority He said, "You will go and do what I tell you to do. You will say what I tell you to say." Suddenly the vision left and there was an anointing release in my body. It was like fire liquid anointing. I ran downstairs to tell my wife what had just happened. She replied, "Yes great. We'll go see Ma Ying-Jeou." That was on Friday. On Sunday, at 8:30 a.m., I was scheduled to go back to the United States. That Sunday afternoon, at about 4:30, a very good friend of ours came to pick us up. She is a very famous fashion designer. Her name is Sabrina Chen. On the way to the airport my bride shared with her the experience that I had. She encouraged us, "You can't leave Taiwan. You have to give him the prophecy to encourage him. This is from the Lord." She also informed us that at 7 p.m., Ma Ying-Jeou was having a rally at Bayling Junior High. Our steps are ordered by the Lord!! (See Psalms 37:23)

We rushed to the location. There was traffic and cars everywhere. We couldn't even find a parking place. Suddenly there was a sister from the Foursquare Church. She approached us and we told her that we were looking for Ma Ying-Jeou, to pray for him. She told us that he was about a mile away from where we were and that she would be more than happy to park the car for us. I grabbed my Bible and the three of us began running through the traffic. There were people everywhere. We were running because I knew that my time was approaching to catch the flight. There were more than thirty-thousand people all over the place. There was a tremendous momentum in the air. Fireworks were going off, people were laughing, celebrating the rally and having fun. How were we going to find the politician, Ma Ying-Jeou in such a tremendous crowd. My flesh wanted to give up but the Spirit of God would not let me. Thank God we reached an area where there were government people and police officers. We looked all the over the place. There were barricades everywhere. We could not go through. The official said to me, "Who are you, what do you want?" I responded, "I am an American and I have a message for Ma Ying-Jeou from God."

The man very firmly said, "You cannot get in without a pass." My wife and the fashion designer said, "This is a pastor from America. It is very important that you let him in. He has a message to give to Ma Ying-Jeou." The man responded, "I am a Christian too and nobody goes through me. Sorry." I backed up three steps, I lifted up my Bible in the air and shouted, "Satan get behind me in Jesus name!" I looked up at the van that was in the center of the circle. The door opened and three officers looked at me and said, "Let him in." God was at work, just like when Moses opened the Red Sea!

They opened the gate and I went in. As I approached the van Ma Ying-Jeou came out, extending his hand to me. He welcomed me with a big smile. I said to him, "Sir, the God of heaven, the Lord Jesus Christ, that made heaven and earth and everything in it, He sent me to you. He says for you to be brave and strong. "I will be with you because I have chosen you to be a mayor of my people in the future. Rejoice! I am the Lord your God, and I shall bring it to pass." He responded to me, "I BELIEVE, I BELIEVE." To my left, there was a camera that zoomed in and recorded every word that was said. He smiled at me and gave me a hug. I remember that there was power in the air and the prophecy that was released to him, strengthened and encouraged his soul. Several hours later I met my flight and we were airborne, back to the United States. The election was not until 14 days later. During this time many people called my home and said, "Bruno's going crazy. We don't want this man to be mayor. We want the other party." My wife was discouraged and began to doubt. She said, "Bruno we're in trouble. What if he doesn't become mayor, we're ruined. We cannot come back to Taiwan."

Two weeks later we received a letter from President Lee's granddaughter from Taiwan. It stated that Ma Ying-Jeou became mayor. He received over 71, 000 votes. More than the other candidates. Hallelujah!! God is faithful. In Amos 3:7 it says, "God will not do nothing unless he reveals it first to his prophets." While I am writing my journey now, it is January, 2007. By the way, this man is full of integrity and honesty. He is a great mentor and leader. He has lots of love and compassion for the fellow man. God said it and it happened and it will happen again. He served Taiwan as a mayor for six years. Praise God. On January 19, 2007 I had the opportunity to visit my angel. As I am writing these final notes, we received an invitation to do a conference in Taiwan. We believe the best is yet to come. I am hoping and praying that God will open a door for me to go see the ex-mayor and we are hoping that he will become president of Taiwan. Even though this is a very sensitive issue and very controversial, we value your opinion. Do you think he can become president?

JAN. 2007 – BRIEF MISSION TO TAIWAN

I am delighted to write these few lines to you, Dear reader. Especially if you are praying for the political leaders around the world. So that we might have peace. You can agree with me that we need our governmental leaders to obey the rules and laws of God. Paul commanded us in the bible in:

I Timothy 2:1-3 I EXHORT you therefore, that, first of all, supplications, prayers, intercessions, and giving of thanks be made for all men; 2. For kings and for all that are in authority; that we may live a quiet and peaceable life in all godliness and honesty. 3. For this is good and acceptable in the sight of God our savior.

I rejoice to write of the events that God gave me while I was in Taiwan. On January 19 myself and my son Peter Caporrimo, an ordained minister, while we were sharing testimonies in a small church in Taipei about my angel, challenged me to go visit him. He wanted me to give him my book and pray for him. Many people were telling me to go and to show him love and warn him not to burn incense or bow to demon gods. I said to them, "Allright, allright. I will go on one condition! If all of us fast and pray for three days." Well, me and many co-workers fasted for three days. At the end of the fast we took a taxi and went directly to the government building. As we approached the building we saw cameras, news reporters and people everywhere. We asked one of the security guards what was going on. He replied, "All these people are here to see the ex-mayor. He is going to give them a medal and a special interview in front of the press. It will be televised all over the nations, because they won the tournament of Taiwan. They are champions. Going through the crowd was not easy. Special favor was upon our life that day. We managed to go into his office and one of his administrators welcomed us into one of the rooms. He stated to us, "The ex-mayor will see you at 4:30." We were very excited and a bit nervous

Dr. Bruno Caporrimo

because without an invitation it is not easy to see such a righteous and powerful man. But I know that it was God carrying me. I was praying within myself, "Lord give me words to say to him." Then the scripture came to my mind in Matthew 10: 18, 19, 20; And ye shall be brought before governors and kings for my sake, for a testimony against them and the gentiles. 19. But when they deliver you up, take no thought how or what ye shall speak, for it shall be given you in that same hour what you shall say. 20. For it is not you that speaks, but the spirit of your Father which speaketh in you.

At 4:30,on the nose, the door opened and the coordinator came in with the ex-mayor. He extended his hand to me and his presence filled the room. His face looked like an angel. He was the most kind and gentle man that I ever had met. I smiled and said, "Do you remember me?" He replied with a gentle smile, "Yes, I remember you. You prayed for me six years ago." I said, "Thank you for receiving me in spite of your busy schedule. I just want to wish you well and say that we are praying for you. Me, my co-workers and the people in America as well. We are hoping and praying that you will run for President in 2008." His reply was, "Thank you. Yes, pray for me." Without hesitation I shook his hand and I looked at him eyeball to eyeball. I said to him, "You are a Catholic Christian and your faith in the God of the bible forbids that we worship or bow to idols." I explained to him that when the Israelites in the bible worshipped God and turned from idols they all prospered and the nation became strong. But when they turned from God they went back to idols and they were quickly destroyed. I also pointed out to him three points. 1. That God is looking for a man that would be faithful to him. Someone who would stand and not compromise with demon gods. 2. Someone who would not compromise with the idols in the land and bow to them. 3. Someone who would not burn incense. God is looking for this kind of man to be faithful to worship him in spirit and truth like King David in the bible. I said, "If you would do so brother, God might give you the keys of Taiwan." I blessed him in the name of the Father, Son and Holy Spirit and In Jesus' name and then I left his presence. Dear friend, the reason I warned him is because Taiwan is a nation where 95% of the people worship idols. The people in the temple tried to control the government leaders by making them bow down and burn incense to the demon gods. I gave him a warning, from one brother to another. Now it is up to him. If he is willing to stand for Jesus Christ, I believe that he will have a great journey and we might see revival in Taiwan. This is my opinion. By the way, dear reader, what is your opinion? What is your vote in this matter? Is he the man for the season or not? Please let me know. I value your opinion and we love to read your mail.

20
FOURTH MISSION TO CHINA

On December 10th, after several days in Hong Kong conducting a crusade at the Great Assembly Church, we teamed up with some co-workers. We filled our suitcases with Bibles and teaching material. We crossed into China to conduct a two-day conference at the Government Cell Church. While I was fasting and praying about whether to go deeper into mainland China or return to the United States, we were approached by a lady named Rachel. She said, "Dr. Bruno, I came from Sun-Sue, about two-hundred miles away. God gave me a vision to come and get you. Would you please come to my city? In one of the villages there is a man that has been chained for twenty years. He is a man possessed by demons." As she explained this to me, the idea of returning to the United States seemed very good and comfortable. My flesh was saying, "Go home." But once again my steps are not to be ordered by me but by the Lord. I replied to her, "Let me pray for a couple of hours." That afternoon as I lay on the couch, the Lord showed me a vision that I was in the back of a bus going deep into China. I told Lydia my vision. The following day I told our new co-worker, "Yes, we will go with you." As I said this to her I felt refreshed and revived by the Holy Spirit. We proceeded to go to the train station. Before my very eyes I saw thousands and thousands of people. Some were sitting, some were standing, and some were with suitcases or their lunches. They were all waiting for the train. About 45 minutes later Rachel told us that we would have to wait two days to get a train. I exclaimed, "This is crazy!" I remembered the Lord giving me a vision the night before that I was on a bus. Fifteen minutes later, we were on a bus. We sat in the back seat of the bus just like we had in the vision the Lord had given me.

Just before evening, we arrived in Sun-Sue City. Rachel took us to an apartment where we met her husband and two daughters. This was to be our five-star hotel. We slept with one blanket and it was cold throughout the night. These precious people live below the poverty level. Over 300 million Chinese live with no built-in gas, electricity, or even a bathroom. If they need to use the restroom in the middle of the night, they either have to go outside or use a dishpan. For hot water they use a thermos. It was December 19th and the weather was cold. Yet that night over 15 people came to have a Bible study with us. The ones that attended had been informed of the prophetic anointing on our lives and were very excited. They requested me to teach on the Holy Spirit. They asked me to teach them how to speak in tongues and prophesy. We noticed the zeal, the desire, and passion to know more about the Savior. We found out that there were 300,000 people in the city, yet only 100 of them were Christians. You can imagine that with so very little teaching available, they saw us as authors and the greatest evangelists in the world. You could see in their eyes the fiery desire. The hunger to have a honeymoon with the master. You could sense their hope to enter into a higher and greater dimension with the Holy Spirit. After a very pleasant meal, we gathered together and began to pray. I taught them Acts19: 1-6 and 1 Corinthians 14:1-5:

Acts 19:1-6
And it happened, while Apollos was at Corinth, that Paul, having passed through the upper regions came to Ephesus. And some disciples he said unto them, "Did you receive the Holy Spirit when you believed?" And they said to him, "We have not so much as heard whether there is a Holy Spirit." And he said unto them, "Into what then were you baptized?" So they said" Into John's baptism" Then Paul said, "John indeed baptized with a baptism of repentance, saying to the people that they should believe on him who would come after him, that is, on Christ Jesus." When they heard this, they were baptized in the

name of the Lord Jesus. And when Paul laid hands on them, the Holy Spirit came upon them, and they spoke with tongues and prophesied.

1 Corinthians 14:1-5
Desire spiritual gifts, but especially that you may prophesy. For he who speaks in tongues does not speak to men but to God, for no one understands him; however, in the Spirit he speaks mysteries. But he that prophesies speaks edification and exhortation and comfort to man. He who speaks in a tongue edifies himself, but he who prophesies edifies the church. I wish you all spoke with tongues, but even more that you prophesied; for he who prophesies is greater than he who speaks with tongues, unless indeed he interprets, that the church may receive edification. But now bretheren, if I come to you speaking with tongues, what shall I profit you unless I speak either by revelation, by knowledge, by prophesying or by teaching?

I began to share with them some of my experiences with the Lord and how He baptized me and took me to heaven. I taught of how, now, I experience this day after day in my devotions. I also shared about the Lord increasing His anointing in my life and my honeymoon with the Holy Spirit. As we went to pray I tried to pray like Paul prayed. Paul said, "Follow me as I follow Christ." I asked the Lord to bring down the same anointing that God had given to Paul some 2000 years ago.

Suddenly the Holy Spirit was present. I began to lay hands on all of them. Some began to cry, some began to worship the Lord and some began to speak in tongues. Some even began to prophesy. I felt supernaturally charged up by the Holy Spirit. The Holy Spirit then inspired me to prophesy and focus on the very last sister. I began to prophesy to her and told her that God was going to give her a rose. While looking into her eyes she said, "Bruno, I want to have a Honeymoon with the Holy Spirit. I want more." She took my hand and directed it to her forehead. Something wonderful happened then. She started to speak in a strange language. She began to sing and worship. Then she fell to the ground and began laughing like a little girl. She began to laugh, "Ha, ha, I'm so happy. I see Jesus." She continued this beautiful,

From Mafia Boss to the Cross

heavenly language. Then she began to prophesy. Within an hour, she was the attraction of the room. Everyone's focus was upon her. Her eyes were closed, her face was lit up, and there was fire all around her. There was a fullness and awesome presence of joy in the room. The Lord visited this little Bible study. We all watched this wonderful Chinese sister who, without exaggeration, was under the power of God for more than 7 hours. She would laugh and then she would change and speak in tongues. She would prophesy and quote scripture from the Bible. This went on all night and into the morning. Soon it was 1:00 a.m., 2:00 a.m., 3:00 a.m. and now my experiences with the Lord, as you have read this book, have been tremendous. You can even say radical. But I had never experienced anything like this lady. She was under the power in such magnitude and for a long time. At 3:00 a.m. I gave up and I went to bed. I woke up at 8:30 a.m. and she was still under the power and anointing. She had been prophesying, singing, quoting scripture and proclaiming heaven's visions. The Lord had taken me to more than 9 nations and I had experienced great moves of the Holy Spirit, but never anything like this. Truly this was the type of experience that you find in the book of Acts2: 3-4:

> Then there appeared to them divided tongues, as of fire, and one sat upon each of them. And they were all filled with the Holy Spirit and began to speak with other tongues as the spirit gave them utterance.

At 8:30 a.m. we were surrounding her and watching her. We were watching this baby Christian being transformed. I was so impressed and thanked the Lord Jesus for bringing me such a distance, to such a different culture. In order to experience that same thing he gave me, sixteen years ago, which he was now giving to Sister Rose. I want to remind you that for seven hours she never opened her eyes. You might say, "Bruno, what are you trying to say to us?" What I am trying to communicate to you is that she encountered the Master for the first time in her life. She got caught up so deep in the spirit and totally fell in love with the Holy Spirit. Not only had she been baptized with the Holy Spirit, but the Lord had taken her spirit to see him face to face. If this were to happen to you, if you were suddenly able to see the master of the universe face to face, you would not want to open your eyes and be distracted. You would probably want more, and more and more. Finally, at around 8:45 a.m., she came back to earth. Her first words were to her fiancee who had been holding her hands for most of the night and morning without speaking a word to her. She calmly opened her eyes, looked at him and said, "I have been in heaven with Jesus. Now that I am back, if you want to marry me, we have to go to my village to tell everyone that Jesus Christ is real." We spent the next 3 hours together, from 9:00 to 12:00. I began to counsel her fiancee Mark. We found out that they had been living together for 8 years, thinking they could never legally be married, because one of them was married before and divorced. After sharing some scriptures with them, I confirmed to them that they needed to be separated for three days. After the three days they were to be reunited through marriage. We found out that Mark was very gifted with the Scriptures. He had been misled by a spirit of religion. We made it very clear to them that they could get married. While we were having lunch they announced to their friends from the local church that they wanted to be married. Suddenly they looked at us and said, "Dr. Bruno please, we want to get married on Christmas day. Would you marry us?" I shared with them that my job was finished. My job was only to restore them. I had to be back in the United States before Christmas and could not marry them. They began to insist. All their friends were so happy for them and they were all crying. I asked them, "Why are you crying?" They said, "We are so happy. We have been praying for them for eight years." Everyone was so emotional and happy that Lydia started crying. I then found myself saying, "Yes, okay, we will stay." Even though we had planned to stay less than two days.

The love of the Lord was so strong for one another that we came to love these people more than ourselves. The feeling seemed mutual. They also seemed to love us more than themselves. Suddenly I did not care if I was back home by Christmas or not. The Lord was doing something wonderful and we wanted to go with the flow. Now we watched these lovebirds, especially Rose. We watched the joy of her being accepted for marriage, after eight years of rejection. That afternoon, after lunch, we found ourselves going to the only church in this large province of 300,000 people. We were told that there were only 100 Christians. As I heard this, I was very disappointed. But it inspired me to stay and to make a difference.

Our prayer lives got stronger. Because nobody owned a automobile, they took us to the church by motor scoter. The church was preparing for their Christmas celebration. We met the minister and his wife, who we later gave the Biblical names of Pastor John and wife Mary. They had both been pioneering the area for 3 years. After introductions, we all kneeled down and began to pray. They asked us if we would go with them to a village 100 miles away. In this particular village was the man who was demon possessed for more than 20 years. Pastor John shared that many people had attempted to reach this man but failed to do so. I responded that we would stay and accompany them. They all rejoiced. On December 20th, 2000, they made arrangements for a van to take us on our journey the following day. That night I advised everyone not to eat. Only to fast and pray. We spent a quiet night in the presence of the Lord with much prayer being manifested.

21
DECEMBER 21, 2000: MISSION TO BREAK CHAINS

The very next day the church managed to get one small van. The 17 of us stuffed ourselves into the van. Armed and dangerous with the power of the Holy Spirit, we began the journey. We passed many farms, countless rice fields, and many small villages. Praise and worship filled the van all the way there. Finally, we arrived at the old village in the early afternoon. The village had very narrow streets. We entered a house that had no front doors. We gathered in this big living room where all the farmers, workers and housewives stared at this Italian-American. There was much tension in the room and you could feel the demonic influence all around us. The owner of the house was sitting down because he was stricken with arthritis. After a small introduction we began to sing songs and make music to the Lord. I opened up the Bible and shared the gospel with them. After the gospel presentation and a short message, suddenly, the supernatural power of God filled the room. All the people in the village were watching me, eyeball to eyeball. Even through the windows people were watching to see what was going to happen next.

I took the oil out of my pocket and looked at the owner of the house. I said, "Sir, God is going to heal you." I anointed his forehead with oil and prayed the prayer of faith. I backed off and the Holy Spirit zapped him. I told him to get up and check himself. He began to jump up and down and shout in Chinese, "I am healed, I am healed!" Suddenly, in the air of the room and all over the village, the fire of God fell. Immediately I watched all the people shouting with joy. They began to come towards me to be anointed with oil. Immediately I led them in the sinners prayer. I asked the Lord to cast his net upon them and catch his fish. Dear reader, there are no words that could express the beauty of the moments I experienced. I watched all the people and some of them were glowing and raising there hands up to praise God. If you had been there offering $1000 for them to lower their hands, they would have ignored you because the Holy Spirit had entered the room. The Holy Spirit had taken over and where he is, there is liberty, healing, identity, relationship and joy. As I looked around, all the co-workers were praying and shouting to GOD. I looked at the papa and said to him, "Take me to the dungeon, I want to pray for your son."

THE DUNGEON

We walked out of the house and into another building. We went through a hallway before finally entering an old room which looked like a dungeon. There before my eyes I saw a Chinese man chained and naked. The room was wet, cold and moist. I found myself looking at him. He looked at me and got into a position like a dog. He began to howl like an animal. I was there without an interpreter because my interpreter was my wife Lydia. Because she was a woman and there was a naked man, she could not enter the room with me. She stood behind the wall. I sensed fear while entering the room. There I was alone and without an interpreter and with a demon-possessed man. For a moment I was afraid. But then the Lord said to me, "Son, do not be afraid. He is more afraid than you are. Rebuke the demons off of him in my name." I stood there and said, "In the name of Jesus, I command every foul demon to get off him in Jesus' name."

Supernaturally, the Holy Spirit came down between the man in chains and I saw with my spiritual eyes the Glory of God fell upon this man in just a matter of ten seconds. I watched the Holy Spirit with the finger of God clean this man from the bottom of his feet to the top of his head. I watched him shake while he was on his knees and I saw the evil forces flee out of his body. Then he looked at me and smiled and said, "I am free." Behind the wall there were 17 co-workers praying in the spirit. The villagers were also praying intercessory prayers. I asked Lydia, "What did he say?" My wife answered, "He is free." I walked up to him with no fear. He kneeled down and was bowing to the Lord, not to me. I called out for his father and my co-workers and I said to them, "He is free, take the chains off."

Mark 5:1-13
Then they came to the other side of the sea, to the country of the Gadarenes. And when he had come out of the boat, immediately there met him out of the tombs a man with an unclean spirit, who had his dwelling among the tombs, and no one could bind him, not even with chains. Because he had often been bound with shackles and chains. And the chains had been pulled apart by him, and the shackles broken in pieces; neither could anyone tame him. And always, night and day, he was in the mountains and in the tombs, crying out and cutting himself with stones. But when he saw Jesus afar, he ran and worshipped him. And he cried out with a loud voice and said, "What have I to do with you, Jesus, son of the most high God? I implore you by God that you do not torment me. For he said to him, "Come out of the man you unclean spirit!" Then he asked him, "What is your name?" and he answered saying, "My name is Legion, for we are many." And he begged earnestly that he would not send them out of the country. Now a large herd of swine was feeding there near the mountains. And all the demons begged him saying, "Send us to the swine, that we may enter in. And at once Jesus gave them permission. Then the unclean spirits went out and entered the swine (there were about two-thousand); and the herd ran violently down the steep place into the sea, and drowned in the sea.

THE LEGEND

I inquired why this man had been put in chains. What kind of family would do this? Why hadn't the police taken action? Their response was, "Twenty years ago when he was a young man, he was very normal. Then he broke the relationship with his fiancee. Her family sent generational curses to him through many witches and idol worship. He received a sweater from them that was cursed. When he put the sweater on, he began to scream and shout and attack the people in the village. Then he would vandalize the village while running down the streets naked. He refused to wear clothes. His family was fearful that someone might kill him after having so much complaining and problems from the neighbors. His father came to a conclusion to bind him in chains. For twenty years he grew worse and worse." The law in China, especially in rural villages, is much different than in America. For twenty years, this man had been without hope.

WHOM CAN I SEND?

I want to share with you what came across my mind. Twenty one years ago, when they put this man in chains, I was still an unbeliever. The Lord looked down from heaven to Garden Grove, California in 1985. He saved me and baptized me with the Holy Spirit. He ordained me and sent me to a mountain in Arizona for five years. He trained me and equipped me with his power. He prepared a marriage to a Chinese lady and then sent me to Taiwan 14 times. He also sent me to China 3 times. All the while, this man had been bound in chains, bound by the devil and crying out to God. Then the Lord brought me back to China. Then, illustrating his divine plan, He allowed us to meet someone from this city. There, we met a powerful group of Christians, went to the village, and set this man free. This shows the vastness of the love of God. Yet we also see the enemy in action. The devil was trying to destroy this man's life and had put him in chains and misery. The family and the man himself had lost all hope. For twenty years, even Christians trying to cast the demons out of this man had failed. It took God twenty years to raise someone up available to do this work.

Dear reader, prepare yourself. Be available for the ones that are bound not only with physical chains but even worse when the chains are in their hearts. The look of this man after twenty years of torment had changed. He had been set free in a very short time and filled with the Holy Spirit. Hallelujah! By the way, there are millions and millions of people around the world in chains. Our ministry is to make disciples for the end time divine purpose of God to set free those who have chains on the outside as well as the inside. I am so grateful to see the mercy and the compassion of the Lord for humanity.

Dr. Bruno Caporrimo

Note from the author: In September 2002, the author went back. There was a woman in chains and darkness for three years. A pitiful situation. But glory to God she got set free also! Now she's having a Honeymoon with the Holy Spirit!

IDOLS TORN DOWN

As they were dressing him, someone came in and took pictures of him. He looked up in fear and was startled so I told the people to not take anymore pictures. I watched them break the chains with a crowbar because the key had been lost. While everyone was praising and worshipping, I looked to the right and saw all the idols of the family's ancestors. I told the mama and papa, "We need to burn the idols". They both looked at us and said, "Burn them." Again, I took the Bible and read Exodus 20:4 and Mark 16:16-17. I declared to them that they needed to be baptized right away. Some people who are reading this book may ask, "Why did they need to be baptized right away?" First, because there was no time to put up a show. Secondly, there was no church for 100 miles. Thirdly, this was a divine opportunity. Fourthly, God was moving there. Fifthly, we needed to obey the Bible, not man. In Acts 2:38 Peter said, "Repent all of you and be baptized in the name of the Lord Jesus."

When he was released from chains, he was set free in the condition that he was in. He had been bound in chains for twenty years. During that time, he had never shaved or cut his hair. He smelled and stunk beyond human imagination. His mother went to get scissors, cut his hair, and cut his beard while others were busy tearing down the idols. Some were also preparing the water where we baptized him. The brother who had been demon-possessed shared with me, "I am deaf in one hear. Could you pray for me?" As I rebuked the spirit of deafness from him, he shouted, "I am healed." I watched 17 Chinese co-workers. Everyone was doing something. We took all the idols and dragon paintings down. Some of the idols smelled because they had been there for more than 50 years. We dragged them outside the village and burned them all.

While the idols were being burnt, others wanted us to pray for them, and to take and burn the idols from their homes. That night, while on the way back to the city, all of us rejoiced for the hundreds who had come to the Lord. God then gave me a revelation about Joshua and the

From Mafia Boss to the Cross

Israelites when they burned down Jericho and all the idols. Throughout the Bible, we can see what happened to Moses, David, Samuel, all the prophets, and the kings when they burned the idols. It was then that the blessings of God came. The Lord hates idols. Idols bring demons into peoples' lives, and homes. Please read the next passages very carefully. Having traveled throughout Asia and China, I have found that many Christians still have a lot of idols and dragons in their homes. This opens doors to demonic influence. Please read my book, "The Invisible War", to give you more understanding of how you can get the victory over the demonic and its influence. It will give you step-by-step instructions and understanding for the purpose of God in your life.

Leviticus 19:4
Do not turn to idols, nor make for yourself molded Gods; I am the Lord Your God.

Deuteronomy 7:25-26
You shall burn the carved images of their gods with fire; you shall not the silver or gold that is on them, nor take it for yourselves, lest you be snared by it; for it is an abomination to the Lord your God.

I believe that in the days to come God will raise up Christians who will not compromise. They will go into China, India, Italy and other parts of the world-- especially America. They will preach and obey the fullness of God and burn all the idols to make Jesus Christ Lord of all. Hallelujah! The news spread fast of the revival that occurred. We were still fired up with the anointing that God had released on us. Without exaggeration, it lasted more than three days. Years ago I took a Hebrew class. Our teacher was a Jewish born again Christian. He was teaching us that when God opened the Red Sea, God baptized all the Hebrews going through the Red Sea. The Israelites then experienced the fullness of the power of God for more than three days. He explained to us that when God opened up the Red Sea that God had come down with more than 20,000 angels. Dear reader, can you imagine how much fire and anointing God released on the Israelites? Many times we read in the Bible that God sent an angel to the prophets and anointed them to bring revival. Now we read in Exodus 14:27-31, God opened up the Red Sea and all night the Israelites passed through. In chapter 15 of Exodus, it shows that Moses and Miriam sang songs and all the people rejoiced for three days. They went to drink the water and the water was bitter because the anointing left them. They began to pray again and God made the water sweet once more. Maybe in your life you feel a little bitter or dry. If so, turn to the Master and let Him give you sweet water.

So now here we are in China and we are celebrating 3 days of anointing because God came down in the village and set a man free. All of us were receiving the overflow. That very night after dinner we went back to the apartment. After resting awhile, we once again were refreshed and the apartment was full of people. That night we experienced that the people in the choir and the church got baptized in the Holy Ghost. The following day was Christmas Eve. That night the church performed a great celebration service. Pastor John and his wife Mary requested that we would do a healing service. They asked us if we would do it in secret because the church was experiencing some monitoring by the government. It was against the rules to have a healing crusade because they were very traditional and formal. They asked me if I would pray in private behind closed doors. I replied to them, "No. We will worship the Lord and let God do the work."

BOUND MAN IN CHURCH

That night the doors were wide open. We started with 100 people but because the news traveled so fast, soon there were over 350 people in the church. There were also many standing outside the door. The congregation was prepared to see the man that had been bound for 20 years. He was sitting in the congregation with his family. He was in his right mind, fully dressed, and acting normal. As we began to worship the Lord, The Lord began to come down in a special way. Then we called out and began to do healing and miracles. Some of you do not know us and you may be wondering how we pray for people. I have learned a lot from Kathryn Kuhlman, Oral Roberts and Benny Hinn.

If you have read their books or watched them on television, then you have seen their style and how they function with the Holy Spirit. I do things the same way. Allowing the Holy Spirit lead. That night, even the government official in charge of monitoring the church experienced the supernatural power of the Holy Spirit. They also accepted us. They invited us to return to do a conference, train and equip people to evangelize other villages.

THE WEDDING

The following day was Saturday. The Lord inspired us to help Mark and Rose have a Christian wedding. After much prayer, we went out to buy the clothing and a dress. Everywhere we went, we saw people coming to Jesus. We preached everywhere. People are truly open when we walk under the anointing of God. We watched the love of this small group as they worked together to make this wedding come to pass. I watched Lydia delegate in detail and help them with this Christian wedding. The people in this city had never experienced a Christian wedding before. That night, the groom confided with me that his father would refuse to come to the wedding because he was against this marriage and against Christianity. Immediately, we went to pray and took action. I asked him to take me to see his family. Upon arrival, he gladly received us. As we had fellowship with him, we found out that he was a retired schoolteacher. After one hour, under the guidance of the Holy Spirit I asked him to read 1 John 5:12,

> He who has the Son has life; he who does not have the Son of God does not have life.

As he read the scripture (I remind you he is a schoolteacher) he put his glasses down and said, "I have no life?" I replied to him that we have an earthly life but that it is limited and that we are disconnected from God. I told him that God sent me here all the way from America because Jesus wanted to come into his life to give him power and eternal life. He looked at me. He looked at his wife and then at the idols he had in his living room. He said, "Eternal life?" I replied, "Yes!" He answered, "Yes, we want eternal life!" There we kneeled, 6 of us, and he invited the master into his heart. Suddenly there was joy in the room.

Dr. Bruno Caporrimo

I watched his son Mark, full of emotion praising God. The following day, Mark's dad came to the wedding. Hallelujah!

The wedding was conducted so beautifully with so much joy being manifest in everyone. The following day we prepared to leave for Hong Kong. As we took the bus, there were many brothers and sisters wishing us well. We were very moved by watching them crying, wave to us, and ask us to come back. I remind you that the Chinese people are the sweetest people in the world. Especially in giving themselves to serving others. We were very fortunate to spend Christmas in China but we were very happy to go back home after three long months in the mission field. We rejoice that God allowed us to spend New Years with our mother church. We came home as usual, burned out, jetlagged and out of place. Thank God that the members of the church, the intercessors, really gave us a great welcome. They were praying for us the whole time. We can truly say that God is good. It is always good to have a home base, where you can rest and recuperate and fill up again.

22
2001: MISSION TO ITALY WITH MORRIS CERULLO MINISTRY

Here is a brief history of Morris Cerullo. Morris Cerullo World Evangelism: he has been my mentor since 1985. I remember when, every year, he would have a world conference at the Sheraton in Anaheim, Ca. Most of the times that I have attended his conference I have served as an usher. Truly I experienced and saw many, many, miracles. I watched lives being transformed and restored. People came to his conferences from more than 175 nations. Also, Morris Cerullo has been a friend of my family. My brother Sal had the honor of working with Morris Cerullo Ministries. He had the opportunity to have a very warm relationship with Morris' family. I'm sure that if you ask him, he can give you a long story about the experiences with this dynamic ministry!

I want to share some of the highlights of the victories and tragedies that took place in 2001 in Italy. I have been very fortunate that God has allowed me to preach the gospel in Italy three times. I can easily say that we have made many, many, friends in the ministry. In Rome, we had the opportunity to meet a man named Luigi Acaglia. He is a cardinal and apostle next to the pope. We had the privilege of fellowshipping with him and he gave us a tour of the Vatican. I remember that year. In April of 2001 I made contact with Vice-President of Morris Cerullo, Mr. Craig Mauro. He encouraged me to set up a crusade in Italy for Morris Cerullo. He replied that since he had been with Morris Cerullo he had never been to Italy. My response was, "Okay. I know ministries in Naples and Sicily that would love to have you. Immediately I went to work. I called my contacts in Rome, Naples and Sicily. They were really happy when they heard the news. They were rejoicing. They responded, "Si, si, si!! We will be more than happy to set up a crusade for Morris Cerullo!" The meetings were set for early June. We agreed that Morris would come to Rome one day, spend one day in Naples and one day in Palermo, Sicily.

The flyers were made. I contacted Naples where we were proclaiming the upcoming crusade in newspaper, television and radio. I was very fortunate that I had the honor and the privilege to work with Craig Mauro. I would have done anything to make the crusade successful. I was caught up in the middle as a mediator. I remember a few days before leaving, Craig Mauro recommended me to take a one way ticket to Italy and come back with Morris Cerullo, after the crusade on a private jet. After the confirmation we packed and we went to Naples. We arrived the night before the crusade. There we met the Senior Pastor and we took a small flight to Sicily. I was full of joy. I was happy and thanking God that I was going back to my homeland where I was born. I left as a small immigrant and now I am going back there with God as an Evangelist! The people in Sicily gave us a great welcome. They put us in a small villa and they cooked us a great Italian meal. After much prayer the church sent a limousine to escort us to the church. As we arrived at church we saw that there were more than 2,000 people worshipping and shouting to the Lord. The stage was set. The momentum was in the air and everything was going great. I was scheduled to bring the message that night. I was to do a healing service and the next day, Morris Cerullo would conduct a leadership conference. I remember, at 6:45 p.m., while we were praying in a circle, I felt spiritually revived. I was ready to take on Goliath! Tragedy was about to take place. My phone rang and Craig Mauro was on the line. He said very clearly, "Bruno, we are not coming to Sicily. We are in France and we came to a conclusion. We are going to skip Italy and go back to the States." Suddenly I felt fear and panic because everything was scheduled around Morris Cerullo. He was to be the top speaker. The churches, they had already spent more than 40,000 dollars in advertising, television and radio. They even paid in advance, 8,000 dollars for a five star hotel. This was for Morris and his two pilots and the co-workers.

From Mafia Boss to the Cross

I got a hold of myself and I quickly responded to him, "What do you mean you are not coming? Craig, don't abandon me." His response was, "Bruno, I'm sorry. We received a few faxes from the local church in Sicily. They told us, "Don't go there because these people are Jesus only. They are not Trinitarian." I immediately responded to him, "These are the greatest people on the earth. Have Morris come here and preach the right doctrine. Please, everything is scheduled around Morris Cerullo". His reply was, "Sorry Bruno, we are skipping Italy." I was looking to find a hole to hide. For the first time in my life I wanted to hide or run where nobody could find me because this rejection was unexpected. It is not that I am anything. Or superior to them. I have been invited to temples, Jehovah's Witness meetings, Mormon churches, even to the mosque. It reminds me of what Paul said, "For the Jew I become a Jew, for the Roman, I do what Roman's do, for I proceed to preach the gospel and to win as many as I can."

I remember sitting the phone down and having over fifty pastors staring at me. I looked at them and said, "Morris Cerullo is not coming." They looked at me shocked. They said, "Why not?" I replied, "He said you people are Jesus only." They looked at me and said, "We don't even know the meaning of Jesus only. What does that mean?" I could see in their faces their disappointment. For the last three months, these people spent every dime they had to make this crusade successful. This was unexpected news. Is it good news? No, it is bad news. Suddenly, from the office right hand corner, the worship leader looked at me from one-hundred fifty feet away and said, "Let's give Dr. Bruno a welcome as he comes to give us the message. The people shouted and gave me a great applause. My spirit was so down that I wanted to run away but there was nowhere to run. As I got in front of the platform, I saw that there were more than 2,000 people, including 40 members of my family whom I had not seen in 40 years. Earlier that day I instructed the ushers to put them in the front row because they were not born again Christians yet.

My intentions were for them to experience the power of God and make a commitment to come forth. As I stood there on the platform I felt so miserable that I couldn't even open my mouth. All I was thinking was that Morris Cerullo and Craig Mauro betrayed me and abandoned me here in Sicily. There were still three days to go and more cities,

Dr. Bruno Caporrimo

including Naples and Rome, for them to do the crusade. Let me tell you, life is not fair but God is good. As I stood there, that very moment became supernatural. The Holy Spirit of God came down and I heard God's voice. He said, "Call the mute and the deaf, I am going to heal them all." The passage that comes to my mind is in Numbers. When one of the Israelite leaders, Cora, wanted to stone Moses and Joshua. Then God intervened. Now God intervened in my life. I didn't ask for it, I didn't expect it and I didn't pray for it. God said, "Call the mute and the deaf." The power of the Holy Spirit invaded my soul. It supercharged me and my arms got bigger and my feet got bigger. The interpreter followed with the altar call and before my eyes, the people came running. More then 35 people lined up. The auditorium was full of the power of God. It was so thick that you could feel it. Within three minutes I touched the people, one by one. I said, "Receive your healing." The people began to open their mouth and praise God. The fire came down and it lasted about three minutes. Everyone that I touched on their ears and throat, they were being rushed on the platform. Immediately the Pastor asked them to give a testimony. Wow, twenty years in the ministry and I never experienced anything so real. People were shouting and praising God. The Lord lifted everybody up so much that nobody missed Morris Cerullo. You see, when God takes over, people rejoice.

A few seconds later a man came running to me with a little seven year old daughter. While he was crying he shouted, "My daughter was born mute and deaf. Please pray for her." I took this beautiful seven year old girl, dressed all in white and looking like an angel, I put her on top of the pulpit and pulled my fingers into her ears. I rebuked the spirit of dumbness and deafness. By the way the power of God was still there, remember, it is the power of God that works in deliverance. While I put my hands on her throat, her father was on the floor crying. I looked at him. I said, "What's your name?" He replied, "Giovanni and my daughter don't hear me." I whispered. I said, "Giovanni, call your daughter." He said, "ANGELINA!!" She quickly responded, "Yes Papa!" Joy filled my heart and everybody was full of joy. I remind you that the majority of these people came here from three or four hundred miles away because they heard on the radio that Morris Cerullo was coming. The majority of them were under the Roman tradition from the Catholic Church. They worshipped many idols and now they were experiencing the true living God. Everyone was filled with the Spirit of God. This included all my nephews and nieces and cousins for whom I have been praying for more than twenty years. Not only me, but many members of my family and my local church. Now I was looking at them rushing to the altar call, saying, "Uncle Bruno touch me. I WANT JESUS." I hope you will rejoice with me as you read this marvelous experience. You might say, "But brother Bruno, Morris Cerullo didn't come. Were you discouraged?" Yes. "Were you confused?" Yes. "Were you oppressed?" Yes. I learned that disappointments and interruptions arrive in the process of living your life. When down times come, I learned never to give up. I learned to never quit. Focus and lean on the Master and He will make your dream come true.

CREATIVE MIRACLE IN NAPLES

The next day six limousines, full of pastors, went to the airport thinking that Morris Cerullo would be there. They waited flight after flight. He never showed. The following day, in middle of June, we were all scheduled to be in Naples for the second conference. More than forty pastors, including me and my wife, got on the plane heading to Naples. Everyone in Naples was expecting Morris Cerullo to conduct the crusade which I scheduled for him. We arrived in Naples in the early afternoon. More than twenty pastors greeted and rejoiced with us. I was the one that had to tell them that Morris Cerullo changed his mind. Some of the pastors were crying and began to say, "How are we going to tell the people here in Naples when many people gave their personal jewelry? Some gave all that they had to sponsor this crusade!" That night the elders took council. The decision was anonymous that I was to bring the message.

Just before 7 p.m. that night, Craig Mauro from Morris Cerullo sent a fax of apology stating that Morris was not feeling well. He said that Morris Cerullo got sick and that they were looking forward to coming next time. He replied, "Morris' wife Teresa, she's Italian and they love Italy. Please accept our apology." The pastors in Naples were disappointed and discouraged. By the way, these pastors have unique ministries. They put their tent in the worst crime areas and they preach the Gospel for thirty days at a time. Being that I was the one responsible for bringing Morris to Italy, I agreed. I agreed with all the pastors that I would stay in Italy for thirty days and preach my heart out every night. I said that they could keep all the contributions to cover the loss. To pay for the expenses of the Morris Cerullo crusade. They were very happy when I said I would be there for thirty days. Now it is 7 p.m., the worship is over and I am to bring the message. There were more than 2,500 people in attendance. Every denomination was there because they televised on radio day and night. There were very large posters that were distributed all over the city. I greeted the people and they responded well. Ten minutes into my sermon a lady jumped up shouting and carrying a little girl in her arms. She was crying and coming towards the pulpit. She said in a loud, piercing voice, with a broken heart, "The little girl has been crippled since birth and has never walked." She asked for prayer for this little girl who was about nine years old. I responded to her, "Bring her here. God is going to heal her." Now that I look back, if I would have waited and been double- minded by saying, "Lady, you're disturbing the meeting. Please sit down." or, "Lady, not now. Miracles don't happen anymore. You see that your daughter is crippled. You need to take her to the doctor or get a wheelchair." But no, I didn't say that. I had Simple faith for her.

With every fiber of my being, I said, "Bring her here, God is going to heal her." You see, this is called faith in action. Not big faith, this is simple faith. That is what Jesus would do. God wants you to have simple faith. How much faith? Enough as a mustard seed. You see, the church needs revival. And revival begins in your heart. Faith without works is dead. Faith in action equals POWER! I took the little girl in my arms and rebuked a spirit of sickness from her. She fell dead on the carpet floor. Under the power of God I continued to pray and, within five minutes, we experienced a miracle. The little girl got up and started running. Immediately everyone began to shout and praise. Everyone was aware of this little girl's condition. That night all the people were shouting for this great miracle. For the crippled little girl. God gave us the victory. Over 200 people received salvation.

THE ENEMY TRIED TO TAKE MY LIFE

The following day, they took my wife and I to Capri Island. We had a marvelous time. We rested for several days and then we began the thirty day tent revival in the little town of Naples called Casoria. In this town 90% of the stores are controlled by the mafia. The police are limited because they do not have enough man power. There is so much corruption, prostitution, smuggling, gambling and hatred among the people. They are always fighting for territories. Many of them claim to be devoted Catholics. Yet they are controlled by the spirit of darkness and idolatry. Dear reader, as you read this story, please pray for Italy. We need revival. Now you know where I am coming from and you should very well know that I was not in the mafia when I was in Italy. In New York City the mafia tried to get a hold of me, but the Lord intervened. He saved my life, trained me and equipped me. Now he has me on a front line in Italy. The war is not physical, flesh and blood, it is spiritual. The enemy is the devil. But some of these people, they are so spiritually blind, they don't even believe the devil exists. Paul declares in 2 Corinthians that the god of this world had blinded the people. The people that ran this crusade gave me a villa. They cooked for us and for 27 days I slept, prayed, fasted and showed up. Night after night the message went out. Jesus saves, Jesus heals. Jesus is Lord. Night after night I preached with no air-conditioning, under a tent with five-hundred people. Every night I would sweat uncontrollably. Every night, at home, I would take my suit and squeeze it and one quart of water would come out. One Saturday afternoon I was teaching on spiritual warfare. Afterwards 200 students would pray intercessory prayer. While we were praying someone called the fireman. Firemen, police, and ambulance came from all over the place. They came rushing into the meeting. We were disturbed by their actions. We said, "What is going on?" They said, "We got a call that there was a fire on the tent." It was the fire of God on top of the tent. They said, "There is no fire here." The fire chief said, "I saw the fire on top of the tent. Are you guys Christians? What's going on here? Who put out the fire?" It suddenly dawned on me, and I said to the Chief Fireman, "God put the fire on the tent and God put it out." I hope you understand that spiritual warfare brings the glory of God into your house. We know that God is a consuming fire. That very night the worship began. I gave the message on "DIVINE HEALING". Just before I finished the message a family jumped up holding a little baby who was about eleven months old. The father shouted, "My baby is born blind. We have come a long way, can you please pray for him." Immediately I commanded him to come up in front. We were all in one accord. I remember that my elder, Dr. Hugh McRae, I called him behind the pulpit. I invited him to pray with me for the little baby. When I laid hands on him, he cried, and kicked and he was not normal. I knew he was being tormented by demons. You might say, "Brother Bruno how do you know that?" You see, the devil attacks the little children and he gives them a lot of fear. Fear causes the immune system and the human spirit to react. This baby was squirming so much that the mother wanted to stop prayer. I turned around and told the crowd of 500, "Everyone pray in one accord." Suddenly the baby was transformed. He was in a trance. He grabbed my hand and pushed it into his forehead in deep child-like meditation. At that moment I felt the gift of healing kick in. Fire was flowing through my hand into his eyes. His father was on the floor, crying and praying. I whispered to his father, "Call your son by name." He said, "SALVATORE". The baby spun his head around to see and, instantly, God gave him two brand new blue eyes. The next night at about 6 p.m., they sat me in the front seat. Prior to the meeting one of the pastors nudged me and said, "Dr. Bruno, three men want to talk to you." I turned around and I looked outside and I saw one little guy and two bodyguards all in suits and hats, smoking big cigars. They were mafia. I said to one of the pastors, "NO, I don't talk to anyone before the meetings. Later" He looked at me eyeball to eyeball and said, "Dr. Bruno, you better talk to them now. Otherwise we will not have a meeting tonight. These are Capo boss mafia". I got up and walked towards them. They had their hands in their pockets. As I approached them, the Capo boss Mateo said to me, "Dr. Bruno, I want to apologize to you." My reply to him was, "Why". He said, "I called you a big phony because I didn't believe you healed the little boy. But when I found out that it was not you it was the Holy Spirit then I knew you were okay. Would you come to my house and have dinner with us." I said, "Sure." He said, "Is tomorrow at one o'clock okay?"

The next day, Luciano Pirozzi my tour guide, was scheduled to take me there but somehow he had a mechanical problem. His sister volunteered and she came to pick us up to take us to Matteo's house. I told her, "At three o'clock I must be back." She agreed to it. We arrived at about twelve o'clock and there were about fifty people there. I went to have dinner and they wanted me to preach to them. The house was packed wall to wall with people. The woman made the most wonderful food. There was fish and shrimp. They had everything. By the way I truly believe that Italian food, homemade, happens to be the best cuisine in the world. This is only my opinion. I hope you take a trip to Italy and you too will find this out. We ate with my Bible open on the table, because the people hungered for the Lord and were asking many questions concerning Christianity. Matteo, the head of the household, and his wife Rosa invited all the neighbors. Everyone was curious to meet me and shake my hand because they heard of the revival meeting we were having night after night. God was moving and these people were hungry for the supernatural. They were determined to see the boy healed. So here I am, people are picking my brain, asking me many, many questions. And on the other hand they were feeding me all kinds of delicious food. Again I would like to give thanks to all the Italian women. They truly know how to put a banquet together. The boy was five years old and attached to an oxygen tank. He had a problem with his lungs and he received a miracle. After we anointed him with oil we laid hands on him.

> James 5:13-14 says: "If anyone among you is sick call the elders of the church and anoint him with oil and the prayer of faith will raise him up from his sick bed."

There was a man in the room who I found out later was Matteo's son in-law. He was in his thirties and very handsome, however, he was spiritually dead. I found out later that he had a habit, like many Italian men, of beating their wives. He looked at me and he said, "I want to give you a kiss, you are Jesus." I replied to him, "No, I am a sinner like you." I remember giving him a scripture and afterward I looked at my watch. It was 3:00 p.m and I told my ministry director, Luciano, that I needed to go. All the people were insisting that I stay. One particular lady was telling me to go upstairs to take down some of the idols that she had on the wall. At about 3:15 p.m., I began feeling spiritually burned out. The oppression in this environment was thick and I ate too much food. I should've cancelled my appointment and taken a nap there. The people would have been more than happy to give me a room. Instead I pressed in, looking to go back to the villa to prepare a message for the night crusade. BUT TRAGEDY WAS WAITING FOR ME.

Dr. Bruno Caporrimo

As I rushed downstairs from the third floor into the parking space, I saw before me a little tiny Fiat. A very, very, small car. I looked in it and there was my wife, Luciano the director and the drivers wife in the back seat. They were waving to me saying, "Come on, let's get in the car. Let's go". I sat in the front seat and said to my director, "Why are we changing cars?" He replied, "The lady had another appointment." I did not feel comfortable with this man driving the car. But I submitted anyway because I learned as a missionary that often things on schedule are subject to change. I did not listen to the Holy Spirit, the small voice inside me. In the next few lines you will understand the situation that I got in. So that maybe you can make a better choice in time of opposition.

The driver smelled terribly with the spirit of nicotine. I went to put my seatbelt on and there were none. By the way, it was about 3:30 in the afternoon and there was no traffic. I remember my wife screaming and saying, "Watch the road." The driver was swerving the car while he was talking to us. He had his right hand towards the glove compartment. He was trying to get a tape because he wanted to bless us with some music. I watched him wiggling with the car. I could not say to him, "Watch the road" in Italian. I said to him, "Let me help you. You drive and I'll take the tape out of the glove compartment." The last thing I can remember is that I looked down to see this Christian tape that he claimed that he had. I'm shuffling and I am looking for the tape. I would never dream that we would get into a wreck because there was nobody on the road. Well, the enemy got a-hold of this guy's mind. He went off the road on the other side at 60 miles an hour, over the sidewalk and he hit a metal telephone pole. I didn't see anything. My focus was in the glove compartment. I heard metal bang. I flew out the window. My hand went into the window first, then my head. The Bible says the devil comes to kill, steal and destroy (See John 10:10). In a matter of seconds my arm was slashed through the glass, my tendons and my nerves were cut. At the present time I have 53 stitches. I was screaming, shouting, and my liver was punctured. My kneecaps were damaged and my head was bleeding and my face was cut. The pain was so tremendous that that day I died for five seconds. In my spirit and in my mind I saw two ugly demons with spears and the worst kind of ugly look. They had evil eyes. They were out to finish me off. I heard the voice of my wife saying,

From Mafia Boss to the Cross

"Jesus, help us." Then the Holy Spirit kicked my soul back in my body. Blood was all over the place.

I fainted for the first time in my life. I passed out. Why do I say that, because I'm tough? No. I say it because this is my autobiography. As you read the story above you see, I dealt with the mafia. In my life before, I was involved in many fights, shootouts, I had been hit with a baseball bat, I had been mugged, I was once almost raped, but I had never been knocked out. And now, I woke up in the hospital. This hospital is located outside Naples. They did not have all the remedies in their medical facility like the surgeons, here, in America. I came to and this Italian nurse was sewing me worse than a shoemaker. I was experiencing trauma, fear, rejection, worry, panic, disappointment and discouragement. All of this got a hold of my head but I remember praying. I sent a quick telegram to heaven. I said, "Lord if they cut my hand off, or my legs or my eyes, NO MATTER WHAT HAPPENS, I WILL NEVER QUIT SERVING YOU LORD."

I admit there was a struggle in my body and in my spirit. They were saying, "You see God doesn't love you no more. He has allowed the accident in your life. You lost your covering." The voice was so loud. I admit that I was disappointed. I was disappointed because for more than thirty days we experienced the blessings of the Lord. Not only me but the people around me. They put me in this World War II hospital. The nurse was nervous. She looked at me and said, "Please pray for me." I said, "Pray for you, aren't you a nurse? It is too late now, do your duty." She said, "Yes, but there is so much blood." Her little voice said, "This is a terrible cut. I don't know whether I am sewing right or not." I said, "Don't they have miracle surgeons here?" She said, "No, not in this village. They come by every other day." In this hospital you got quick help if you were connected. Fortunately, Luciano Pirozzi's brother happened to be the mayor of the city called Luciano. A few minutes later there he was with the police. He told everyone that I was a special friend. They sewed me up and put a twenty pound splint on my hand and an arm. They patched me up and put me in the room. The pain was beyond what I could bear. The doctor gave me pain shots.

Several hours later at about seven or eight the doctors all got together because they knew I was a healing Evangelist. They all rushed to the room along with the nurses and the director. One of the doctors said, with the spirit of criticism, "Aren't you the healing evangelist? Look at you now. Where is Jesus now? You said that God heals people, hah, hah, you see, now you need us!" The man was very critical but in a way he was right. We do need doctors by all means. Jesus said in the epistles, "The sick need a doctor." When the Lord said that, He proclaimed technology all over the world. He proclaimed that we do need doctors. My philosophy, even now, is that we need Christian doctors, Christian lawyers, Christian presidents, Christian mechanics, Christians everywhere. I responded to the doctor, "You can sew me up, stitch me up, but you can't heal me like Jesus." I also replied, "You are a great doctor. I do respect you and salute you. I am in tremendous need but bear in mind, dear sir, that Jesus is the only Universal doctor and King of Kings and Lord of Lords."

On the second day, I remember lying down and I was listening to the sound of the patients that were coming in everyday. Some were in serious trauma while screaming and crying. The majority of them were praying to Mary, the mother of God, or to their favorite saint. I'm lying there meditating, "How did this happen to me?" Suddenly, to my left, someone nudged my arm. I looked to my left, and there before my very eyes was the man driving the car. He was kneeling down praying, with tears coming out of his eyes. I looked at him. He looked like an Angel. My heart reached out for him. Through my struggle and my pain he opened up his mouth and said, "Forgive me, I should have been in your place. Not you." He said, "I have no insurance. Please don't call the police. They will put me in jail. But I have a friend who looks like me, were going to exchange licenses. So the insurance company can compensate you." My response to him was firm. I said, "No, but I do forgive you. So, don't take this to heart anymore." You must say, "Brother Bruno, what about your damages, what about your handicap for life. Don't you want to receive benefits?" My dear friend, I learned one thing. When you forgive the healing comes faster and God will send many blessings to you. Not only did I forgive him but I had the privilege to lead him to Christ. For the twenty one days that I was in that hospital his wife, including Matteo's wife, would visit me three times a day.

WHAT THE DEVIL MEANT FOR EVIL, GOD MEANT FOR GOOD

Romans 8:28, "And we know that all things work for the good for those called in Christ Jesus."

The church and the leaders were trying to hide the accident from the people. They were sending messages to the hospital saying, "Why don't you leave right away so you get better medical care in the States. They said, furthermore, we don't want people to know that you were in a car accident. It does not look good for us. For five days they were pressing me to leave. But I prayed. I would get up at four o'clock in the morning and go find a quiet place. In spite of my pain, I would read the Bible for two hours. The Lord is faithful. He would anoint me morning after morning, fresh. After my devotion, He would anoint me with fresh oil. For the duration of the twenty one days, here are some of the things that would happen; the driver and Matteo, and his wife Rosa brought more than 200 people to me. They brought family and neighbors to visit me. They loved me. They took care of me and prayed for me. They brought me clothing and food that was cooked fresh daily. I lacked nothing. While at my stay in the hospital, 200 members of the mafia and Matteo's family, came to know Jesus. On the twenty first day the doctor had to reopen my stitches because two of my tendons and nerves were disconnected. I repeat that, the religious leaders, they were trying to cover up my tragedy.

Morris Cerullo did not keep his word. By abandoning me and his commitments, I found myself in a very horrid position. I spent twenty seven days serving, to make up the financial loss, to pay somebody else's debt. Night after night I preached my heart out. My suit had salt spots because I perspired so much. Now the doctor pushed me to have another surgery. After being in that hospital for twenty one days everyone knew that I was a preacher. I remember that one morning the doctors were making rounds. One of them said to me, "Why don't you pray to Mary like we do? Why is your religion so different?" I responded to him with a parable. I said, "Let's go back 2000 years. Let's assume that you are Peter, I am Mark, you are James and he is Matthew and the nurse is Mary, the mother of Jesus. And all of us, we go to Mary in prayer. What would Mary say?" Everyone was listening to me. It was really, really quiet. God is giving me the opportunity to do something beautiful for these doctors. I told the nurse, "Please sit down and let's say that you are Mary, the mother of Jesus, and we all kneel down and pray to you. What would you say?" She responded very firmly, "I would slap all of you in the face." I said, "You see, that's what Mary would say right now to all of us." Somehow, these very brilliant doctors were receiving a revelation. They responded altogether, "I see, I see, Dr. Bruno, we are not going to pray to Mary anymore. But who should we pray to?" I opened up my bible to Romans 10:9-10. It declares, "Whosoever calls upon the name of the Lord shall be saved."

They responded, "We want only Jesus." Alleluia. By the way, I want to express my deep gratitude and thanks to my wife for washing and cleaning me everyday that I was hospitalized. And my sincere thanks to all the Doctors and the nurses. Thank you to all my friends that supported me through my recovery. At the present time Matteo and all his family are attending a very well balanced church in Naples. Matteo is an elder Deacon. As I returned back to the States, with a fifty pound cast on my arm, the members of my church welcomed me with a open heart. The healing is a slow process. Now it is 2007 and still, in my hand, I only have 60% functioning of it. Life is not fair but God is good. I learned that in spite of what life throws at me, downtimes or good times, not to quit. I hope you like this poem:

YOU MUST NOT QUIT

When things go wrong, as they sometimes will,
When the road you're trudging seems all uphill,
When the funds are low and the debts are high,
And you want to smile, but you have to sigh,
When care is pressing you down a bit....
Rest if you must but do not quit.
Life is queer with its twists and turns,
As every one of us sometimes learns,
And many a fellow turns about
When he might have won if he stuck it out.
Don't give up though the pace seems slow...

From Mafia Boss to the Cross

You may succeed with another blow.
Often the goal is nearer than
It seems to a faint and faltering man;
Often the struggler has given up
When he might have captured the victor's cup;

He learned to late when the night came down
How close he was to the golden crown.
Success is failure turned inside out.....
The silver tint of the clouds of doubt,
And you never can tell how close you are,
It may be near when it seems afar;
So stick to the fight when you're hardest hit,
It's when things seem worst
That you must not quit...

23
2001, SEPTEMBER
END TIME MISSION TO ASIA

While my arm was recovering by God's law of nature and the natural healing process, I was seeking the Lord. The Lord reminded me that many, many people are dying and going to hell. He reminded me that I need to get up and go. We organized a 90 day mission to Taiwan, Hong Kong and mainland China. At our arrival in Taiwan we rejoiced to see my wife's family and many co-workers and friends. They all sympathized with my injury. Some of them invited me to go to health and massage doctors. Chinese people are known for massages and herbal remedies. Within three weeks we conducted a school of ministry for three days in evangelism and we experienced revival. Taiwan is the first and the largest idol worshipping nation in the world. The second is India and the third is the Catholic Church which is idolatry and abomination in the sight of God. In The Ten Commandments, found in Exodus 20:1-4, it declares; "I am the Lord your God and I am a jealous God. You shall have no idols before me or make an image which is in heaven or below the earth." Theologically this is true. And this is the way of life that God has for children. When we disobey God then the people and the nations suffer. The time was coming up for us to go to Hong Kong. We were received by a Chinese brother. His name was Pastor Abraham. We agreed to give him thirty days of our time to go to Hong Kong. In Hong Kong, 90% of the people are idol worshippers. They inherited it through their ancestors. Hong Kong is a very unique place. The people are very sweet and the city and the culture are stunning. It is wonderful there. It is a wonderful place for sight seeing. The British have built an empire. The structures, the city and the buildings are well established for all generations, around the world, to enjoy. I hope that you will visit someday.

Pastor Abraham has a small church in the center of the city on the sixth floor, with no elevator. We conducted revivals which were open to the public and in the daytime we were increasing with many students enrolling day after day in the School of Evangelism. One of the reasons for this revival, was that the Lord would wake me up every morning at 4:00, I would pray and have devotion everyday until seven in the morning. I remember this particular morning like it was yesterday. My brother Joe was hospitalized prior to my leaving for the mission. He was in a coma. Every morning, on my knees, I would pray for Joe. This very morning, God, through the gift of discernment would give me a vision that two Angels took Joe to heaven. God said, "Be strong and be firm. Continue to be a laborer of love." That very morning I confronted my students in the class. I indicated to them that my brother passed away. There were thirty students and they all responded, "We'll give you the money. You need to go to his funeral right away." I said, "No, no, I'm not going to the funeral. My brother is not there anymore. Jesus said to let the dead bury the dead, you go preach the gospel." That very afternoon we received a phone call from Hugh McCrae, the elder at my church confirming that my brother had passed away.

TRIBUTE TO MY BROTHER JOE AND FAMILY

Joe was the leader of the family. He was very bright, strong, and a champion in his character and abilities. I remember when we were small, right after the war. Joe would put me on his shoulder and he would climb the mountain of Monte Pellegrino. This mountain is very touristy and one of the wonders of the world. This is also where the Germans took a stand against the Americans in the second world war. This is my tribute to Joe, Joe's family, my niece and nephews. Joe would climb the mountain and pick sacks of almonds and prickly pears. Other times, early in the morning, he would go pick snails. He would sell them in the market or to the American soldiers who were stationed there. In return he would get money to buy food to feed a family of seven. Joe was only about eleven years old. He was always a leader and provider for the family. I remember three years before this, that he had a tumor in his brain. He was not supposed to live and Lydia and I fasted for three days. We went to the hospital and my wife laid hands on him and God healed Joe. God gave him three more years of life. Joe was a Navy man. He lived for one purpose, to make provision for his family. Before he passed away his three children, Mark Anthony, JoJo, and Rosanna, were all blessed and married. Joe fulfilled his mission on the earth. Even though the enemy cut his life short, God gave him eternal life.

Now I am 10,000 miles away from the funeral. I want to be there to comfort my sister- in- law and my niece and nephews, however, my time and my calling did not permit. I cherish the many memories and the fun that I had with Joe and his family. I wish I could have been at the funeral to hug them and to express my sympathy. Life is not fair but God is good. Joe cannot come back to us anymore but someday we'll go to him. Joe, at the present time, is walking on the streets of Gold because the ship sailed and reached the final destination and he received an eternal crown. I learned to compromise when facing a contradiction. I was stuck in a rut, whether to stay and continue my mission or go to Joe's funeral. I had already made up my mind.

The revelation that God gave me in devotion, this was the creative insight which appeared. In the form of a bright idea, it came in, and taught me how to change my mind. How to break free of my ego. I felt the Holy Spirit's leading. The idea was that people who never change their mind are either perfect or stubborn. I know I am not perfect. I don't want to be stubborn. So my ego was redeemed and I was liberated to see and hear the alternatives. Other controversial opinions, viewpoints and interpretations. You see, we can move from emotional immaturity to emotional maturity. When we are willing to amend and compromise some of our narrowest ideas and most hardened opinions. If you want to learn and grow you have to admit that you don't have all the correct answers. If you want to succeed you have to listen to the problems and criticism that others have of your ideas. This is one of the principles that I have learned to live by. I don't want my own way. I want to be successful!! I don't want my own way, I want to do the right thing. Positive compromise is being willing to humble yourself. It leads to genuine integrity of character. It brings true identity and liberates from gossip and faultfinding. Positive compromise swallows a lot of pride and absorbs a lot of hurt. Compromising is lowering yourself to listen to people who are smarter than you. So you can learn from them. Positive compromising goes behind the present moment to the big picture that God inspires. In times of tension in your work, in your marriage, or relationship between you and others, focus on positive compromise by looking at the big picture. The one that the Lord has given you!! Abraham Lincoln ran for president 17 times and lost. He was put in a mental hospital for 2 years. Then the big picture came. The Lord answered. He became the greatest president that America ever had. Positive compromise is learning to let go. Letting go is a powerful universal principle. Instead of saying no try letting go. Let it go for good and for now and let go to avoid a painful ending. Compromise when you must but don't throw away your destiny. Learn to let go by thinking further ahead or thinking bigger.

I remember the struggle and commotion that was happening prior to the meeting. A lady who was 82 years old, she was carried in a wheelchair six floors, because she heard that God was healing people. That very night, after my message, we invited the people to be healed. This 82-year-old lady got up and started walking and she testified that she was a second generation Christian. She asked us, if we would go to do healing service in China. She said, "I have a contact. I will schedule the meeting for you because China needs the experience of this healing anointing." She also contributed some money for us for the journey. Seven of us, armed and dangerous, with bibles and books crossed the border of China. The police customs opened my bag and found forty copies of "The Snake in the Glass." They interrogated me. I took one of the books and gave it to them. They wanted to know my profession. If I would have said that I was a preacher they would have stopped me. In my heart I said, "Lord put words in my mouth." I said, "I am a doctor and I teach the Chinese people not to drink alcohol." He looked at me and then he looked at the book. He said, "Very good, very good. We need doctors like this. In China, too many people drink." He said, "My father is an alcoholic." I said, "Take another book." 'The Snake in the Glass', that I gave him was in Chinese. We arrived in a city called Sing-Jing. Pastor Philip, who was 88 years old, was our tour guide. That night over 2,000 people packed in the church under the banner of Chinese Communism. These were people who never experienced divine healing. That night my bride Lydia sang a few songs and supernaturally the Holy Spirit moved in that place. We had more than 60 people come to the platform and testify of their healings. Pastor Philip was full of joy and weeping like a baby. He said, "Dr. Bruno I have been waiting more than 50 years for this in China." If you would like to see the pictures of this event see our website.

CHAINED WOMAN SET FREE

Several days later, Mark and Rose and some of my co-workers came to join us. These were my co-workers from previously. When the man in chains was delivered. After spending some time in fellowship with them they informed me that there was a woman in chains. They instructed me that she had been bound in chains for four years already. They stated that the governor and her father put her in chains outside a remote village. They told me that she was demon possessed and that she had broken many chains before. She would go into rampages and walk around naked like an animal. They challenged me and asked me to go there to minister to this woman. I accepted the invitation. I asked them to join with me in a fast for forty eight hours. On the third day, after a long journey, we went into a village near Sun Sue. At our arrival I instructed 18 co-workers and the local pastors, Mary and Joseph, to take their positions around an abandoned house. They did and they began to pray. A short time passed. We entered the house and before my very eyes there was this beautiful woman kneeled down in a squat position, chained at her stomach, hands, and feet. There was a very large, wooden bed, with no mattress and all the surroundings smelled from her human wastes. The place was beyond remedy. I was shocked and horrified all at once. How could anyone live in these conditions? The walls were gangrene. Looking at her, my heart began to break. I wanted to reach out to her. Form the depths of my being I cried out to the Lord for His power and His anointing. That it would manifest in this woman's life. The Bible tells us in the book of Mark that there was a man who was demon possessed and that no one could bind him. He even broke chains. But now this is not a man. This is a gentle, sweet, woman. Our hearts reached out for this lady. I was told that many missionaries went there before and the responses were all in vain.

The violence and the action of this woman with chains was immense. She would push people back. After much prayer we began to sing songs. With two interpreters, English to Mandarin, Mandarin to Cantonese, the lady responded to us very negatively. I said to her, "I am a doctor. I came from America to take your chains away." She replied, "No, no , don't take my chains away. Go away." Dear reader, what would you have done if you were there? She's telling us to leave. I had with me more than ten women. I began to give a testimony. I read the Bible and people prayed in the spirit. The women were trying to put clothing on her. She even refused to be dressed. We asked her mother to give us the keys so we could remove the chains. Her mother said that the keys were lost along time ago. I asked my co-workers to go to the village to get chain cutters. We began to cut the chains off. We cut chains from her feet, her stomach and her hands. The whole time she was screaming, hollering and kicking. The whole thing was dramatic. I thank God that this time I had a live video. We captured most of it and we have a dvd available for you. We also want to express our warm thanks to Paul Crouch for the editing work.

Well, time went on, and after much struggle I took a bucket of water and I put some olive oil in it and we prayed and cried out to God for the transferring anointing and now that we look back, on the video, we can se the Holy Spirit coming down with our natural eyes! Dear friend, you don't want to miss this. You need to see this video. It will be a life changing experience. I then baptized her and incredibly, before her very eyes, she smiled and stood up. Suddenly she was transformed by the anointing that God released into her life. She smiled at us. There is something about water baptism. She came out fresh and brand new. With more struggles she got dressed. She needed medical attention because her feet and hands were scarred from the chains. We got the little money that we had, more than 1,000 dollars, and took her to the nearest hospital 60 miles away. We checked her in and we found out that there were 100 women in that hospital that had been brought up in abusive homes. All my co-workers and my wife and I had the opportunity to preach the gospel to all of them. Our little friend got a nice bed, a safe place to sleep for thirty days. We took our victory home with us and came back to the States.

Two years had gone by. We wanted to know if she was okay. I prayed and I was getting no response. In 2004 we went back to the village and there she was. Totally healed! God totally restored her. She was the highlight of the day. We took the video with us. Her and her family and friends came to Christ. We fixed the apartment and she's now living with her son. She is living a normal life, free from her chains. She now only has a physical scar to remember. The scar is our trophy for the Lord Jesus. You might have some scars in your life but remember Jesus has them on his hands and his feet. He did it for us all!! He took our pain when he did not know pain. Someday very soon, we will see him face to face. So we must remember that life is not always fair. But GOD IS GOOD.

From there we flew to Malaysia. We ministered to the Full Gospel Chapters, Chinese and English speaking. Several days later one of the local Churches took us 90 miles to a city called Ipoh. There we spent thirty days with an Assemblies of God Church, Pastor Abel and family. The Lord did many marvelous things with so many people coming to Christ. I remember one day we went to a hospital to visit a lady who had a liver problem. She was full of poison and the doctor gave her three days to live. A lady named Dacos took us to the hospital. We arrived there at 3:00 p.m. Ninety percent of the workers in that hospital were Islamic in religion. Again, the hospital looked like it was built in 1920. There were sick people in every area. There were people waiting in line, people waiting in elevators and in the hallways. As I walked in with my oil and my Bible in my hand everybody took notice of us. We got to the patient's room. By the way, in faith we went in. We believed that the Lord would heal the person we were praying for. We opened the door and there was a lady who was about 45 years old. She was breathing very heavily with a very hot temperature and her body was turning green from the sickness. I was introduced to her. She nudged, barely looking at me and focusing her eyes. We began to sing songs. Everybody in this big, large room was looking at us. "What is this crazy guy singing for. This lady is dying." I noticed everyone was looking at us but we continued in the faith. We began to sing to the Lord. I took my oil and anointed her and began to rebuke sickness away from her. First Peter 2:24 declares, "By the stripes of the Lord Jesus Christ we are healed." Psalms 103:1,2,3 declares, "Bless the Lord all my soul, bless his Holy name, who forgives all our iniquities and disease."

While we were praying and anointing her with oil, suddenly, there formed a circle of people all around us. They looked astonished. They were being drawn in by the Holy Spirit. I led them to a sinner's prayer. They responded very well. I left that hospital thinking, "Is she going to recover or is the Lord going to take her home?" I admit my faith was very small. I was thinking that she was at the point of death. The second night at about 7:30, while the worship was going on, there were more than 300 people in attendance. I looked at the front row and the patient from the hospital was standing there. The Lord did heal that lady. Praise God. She left the hospital and came to the conference and gave a testimony. But this is not the end of it. Several days later I was asked if I would go 50 miles away to a village where there were 400 families. I accepted the offering. We took off. The tour guide driving us arrived at the village. I noticed that every home had idols in the front yard. When we arrived at the family that we intended to go, to my surprise, it was the same lady that had come out of the hospital. She came rushing out of the house with her husband. Her husband was about 70 years old. He was a very skinny man. He said, "Thank you , thank you. You healed my wife and last night I saw an Angel at my house." Very aggressively he said, "Please, I want to be baptized right away. I want Jesus." We went inside the house and we sang some songs. I gave him an invitation to accept Christ and I baptized him in the water. This is a man that had

been worshipping idols for 60 years. There were idols all over the house. I responded to him, "These are your enemies. God hates idols." He turned around, full of faith, saying "Dr. Bruno destroy them all and burn them." For three hours we tore down all the idols. These people burn fake money to their ancestors so there are always ashes in a stockpile. It took us three hours. We filled up sacks and took them outside of town to the dump. The Bible says, "Be gentle as a dove and sharp as a serpent."

While I was going in and out of the house I noticed, in the front property, that there was a 4 foot idol of Buddah. I kicked it with my foot and I began to break it down. Suddenly the next door neighbor screamed and shouted, "What are you Americans doing. This is my god and my temple, it belongs to me. Why are you destroying my God?" This man not only rebuked me, he began to rebuke the people who were just baptized. I found out that it was his brother who lived next door. This man had allowed his brother to put the Buddah in his front yard. I assumed logically that this was another altar that belonged to him. When the man's anger rose against him he was like a Goliath and I was like a midget. I was guilty. I shrunk down to a midget stature and I apologized to him. I found myself putting the altar back.

Warning: to anyone that likes to tear down idols in temples,

Rule #1, do not be afraid of the idols.
Rule #2, always go for the souls of the people to be saved.
Rule #3, when people say they are baptized in the Holy Spirit then, automatically, they give you the permission to tear down the idols.

In my instance, I had the permission, so I thought I was doing the right thing. The man was very, very, angry. He was screaming and hollering. I walked away and began to pray. Five minutes later I went into his house and I said "Please forgive me for breaking the idol. Here is 200 dollars, please repair the idol." The man looked at me with his wife and daughter standing there. He saw that I had compassion. He responded, "No, no, don't give me the money. I understand that my brother is a Christian, but I am not, and I know that Jesus healed my sister. We saw the miracle of God in their life."

We left Malaysia and returned back to the United States. We were so exhausted and jet-lagged that I coughed and lost my voice for three weeks. My wife went through a life change. She ended up in a hospital for seven days. She was coughing and peeing in her pants from the bad water and the

dust and pollution in China. The Bible declares, "Many are the afflictions of the righteous, but God delivers from all." Within 30 days we recovered. You might say, "Brother Bruno aren't you tired? Aren't you exhausted?" Yes, often. But God made the human body that, at night, it could be so exhausted. But when you get up in the morning and you've had enough rest you get up and go build your dream. Jesus commanded us in Matthew 28:19-20 to go all over the world and make disciples. You might say, "But Bruno I have no time. I'm having fun. I have my career and I want to enjoy life." You can enjoy the pleasures of life. The Bible declares in the first book of John that the love of money, the love of the world, and the lust of the eyes eventually will kill you. You might say, "Well I will wait until that happens, right now I am having a good time."

I once did all those things. Because I was not of Him but now I got caught. I belong to Jesus and God chastised me. He gave me a spiritual spanking. If you belong to Him then God will correct you and chastise you. Just like a father loves his son, he corrects him and spanks him. After a good spanking there is lot's of joy. There is an awareness to do the right thing and not to make the same stupid mistakes again. Many things that we do wrong in life are not God's fault, or our neighbors fault, or the other guys fault. The enemy works on our ignorance. The Bible is very specific. It says get wisdom and get knowledge and understanding. For instance, there are many things in my life I have allowed. It was not the devil. It was me and my flesh, because I lacked knowledge. The law in California is that you must have seatbelts on when driving. Why? Because seatbelts save lives, especially when a car hits something or another vehicle going 70 miles an hour. The impact is so great that you would fly like a bullet out of the car. How do I know that? Because I have been in five car accidents. Not one time was I driving and yet I have been driving more than 40 years. I have been fortunate. But I lacked wisdom in this area because I trusted a bad driver. Sometimes we don't think clearly enough or take the time to investigate something. It is because we allow ourselves to be in the fast lane. The driver in Italy had no seatbelt in the car and no insurance. If I would have asked him I would not have gone in the car. I would have saved myself a lot of trouble. Maybe this could be a lesson to you. You might say, "I am a Christian." "Well, do you obey the laws of the land? Do you obey the laws of the highways? Do you have insurance in your car? Are your tires in good shape or are they worn out?" You say you are a Christian but yet you are endangering yourself and others on the highway. Then you insist you want to take people for a ride. I am saying this not to condemn anyone but I am saying this so it can be a eye-opener to you. Jesus said in John 15:7, "If you love me you obey my teaching, and if you love me you obey the laws of the land. If you obey the laws of the land then no one can accuse you because you are doing a good thing. By doing this you keep the law and defend the law." Jesus is the law. The word law means to point the way. In John 14:6 Jesus said, "I am the way the truth and the life."

At the end is eternal life. Jesus promised, "He that believes in me, even though he dies, he shall live." So I say to you, let Him catch you and He will set you free. John 8:36 declares, "He that God sets free is free indeed." There is only a small price to pay compared to what is waiting for you and me after our departure. There is great wealth, eternal life and great riches in Christ Jesus. Go on, let Him give you a dream and a vision and get the provision. No matter what it takes. He will give you wisdom to think right and do right. You don't have to be a slave anymore, a slave to sin. I remember the words in the epistles where Paul says in Philippians, "I forsake all the past and press on to the mark of the high calling of Christ Jesus our Lord."

24
DECEMBER 2004: INVITATION TO N.Y.C.

I remember that in 1972, the District Attorney ordered me out of New York City. The declaration was made that I was the number two jewel thief in America. I didn't know then but I know now that God was in control of my life. Proverbs 29:26 declares that 'God is the one that judges the case.' So you see, it was God that took me out of the mafia. God brought me out of California and God chose me to serve Him. Now thirty years had gone by and the doors opened for me to go to Flushing, New York to minister to a Chinese congregation and Pastor Helen and Sister Heaven. They heard that I did much ministry in Taiwan and Asia. They organized a four day conference. There are many, many people sick in the church and there are one million people of Chinese descent in Flushing who do not know Jesus. "We heard your testimony and we told them about you. They want to see what a mafia guy looks like. Would you please come?" I accepted the invitation. Much prayer was made prior to my leaving because I confess that, as a human being, I was a bit nervous to go back to New York City. But on the other hand there was a part of me that was excited because I left there as a law breaker. Now I am going back with the law of God in my heart.

At my arrival in New York City there was excitement in the air. It was exciting to be there. The Chinese people really gave us a treat. Night after night I gave lectures and shared my testimony. Many, many people believed the Gospel. We met very strong Christians and very weak Christians. There was a man in the meeting who was taken by a stroke. He said, "I know who you are. I read your book, 'Invisible war'. I have been waiting for you. I believe God is going to heal me." That night we prayed for him and God gave him a new heart. There was such a move of God there. They extended the meeting for another three days. New York City is one of the best cities in the world. Over 160 nations of the world reside there and call it home.

EXPENSIVE IDOLS THROWN OVER BROOKLYN BRIDGE

New York City is very famous for crime life. As I mentioned earlier in the book, there are five mafia families controlling the territories and there are a lot of dark, shady deals. When the youth or the gangs commit crime, to get rid of the evidence, they would destroy it by throwing it over THE BROOKLYN BRIDGE! I admit that even myself a long time ago, after shoot-outs, would throw guns over the bridge. I thank God that I never killed anyone or never robbed someone's home. NEVER! I always believed that home was the domain of a king. Even though I was deceived and corrupted, I kept this rule. I have been blessed that the Father has turned me around. In more than twenty years I have gone through a lot of pain, trials, and much drama in my life. But it is a small price to pay compared to what Jesus went through and all the people before me. I remember that life is not fair but God is good. Paul the apostle begins in the book of Romans 1:1, "I am a servant and a prisoner of the Lord Jesus Christ, and the father that called me to preach the good news."

Wow, what a privilege, what an honor to serve the living God. The Lord gives anyone a new identity through His redemption. Remember, my philosophy is: To serve the Lord Jesus Christ and to be a Christian IS FUN!! REMEMBER THIS!! For more than twenty years GOD has transformed me. Do it with positive thinking and you will get fun. In Romans it says that God is love, peace, and joy in the Holy Ghost. Did you know that the word Joy is short for Christ. You cannot have joy in life without Christ. Religion separates but Joy restores. Would you like to have some joy? Then turn away from sin and come to Him who takes

From Mafia Boss to the Cross

away the sting of sin and gives you the ring. If you want this then you got to give it all, to get His all. To get all that He has now.

In the second conference that we were conducting, they gave me an interpreter named Linda. I can easily say that she is full of life, full of the spirit and she loves people. She also came out from mafia oppression. Linda is Chinese and she was born in Taiwan. She has resided in New York City for many, many years. She loves people. She hates crime and violence. God truly has transformed her life and she has a great ministry among the Chinese community. On the second night of the meeting she brought a gentleman to us. He said, "Hello, my name is Simon Tu." This man is one of the top, famous, jewelry designers in New York City. Any fashion show that is international, they always use Simon. He recently designed the jewelry for President Chen's daughter in Taiwan. That night my message was, "Spiritual warfare and destroying and taking down idols".

Right after the meeting I was told by Linda that Simon Tu wanted to take us for lobster dinner. We accepted the invitation and brother Simon asked me many, many questions. He mentioned to me that his father and himself and his family had been worshipping idols for many, many years. He also mentioned to me that he had over two million dollars in idols in his uptown, Eastside New York City apartment. He kindly asked me if we could go there and remove the idols. The following night, Linda, Rose, Simon, Lydia and myself, we arrived at his apartment. Before my very eyes we saw all these expensive idols. Bear in mind that I used to be a jewel thief. Now I am in a different business. I tear down and destroy the idols for the Glory OF GOD. You might wonder at this point, "Why do you need to do that?" There is one thing, the worst thing, God hates and that is idols. Even American Idols! Exodus 20:1-4 declares that God is a jealous God. Who are we to provoke God? WHO does America think it is? Or CHINA, or ITALY, or THE VATICAN? They have made a mockery of God by allowing each nation to become idolatrous. I thank God for his spankings. Spanking gives healing and restoration to the soul and to the Nations. I briefly would like to say that God blessed the Israelites out of Egypt and out of the idols. The Israelites, now called Jews, were blessed for thousands and thousands of years but when they allowed the idols to come back in, they welcomed Satan. They allowed the demons to have a foothold on the earth and they received punishment for their disobedience. This is a lesson that we need to learn. Especially in America. It is becoming a nation of idolatry. I hope and pray that America comes back to God in the fullness. My motivation is to please God the Father and his Son, my Chief-in-Commander, the creator of all things.

God has a sense of humor!! One time I sold jewels under the hand of Satan. Now I steal the idols from the very hand of Satan. If we all do this then we can clean up this nation. By the way, always obtain permission from the people. Brother Simon said to me, "Dr. Bruno, I read your book, 'Invisible War'. It is true that idols bring demons into my life and my home. I have been having bad dreams and nightmares." If you want to know more about the effects of idols, that cause the nations to suffer, then get our book, "The Invisible War". I can easily say that God is true and the word of God is the way of life.

Deuteronomy 7, 25-26,
The Graven Images of Their GODS Shall He Yeah Burn with Fire: Thou Shalt Not Desire the Silver and the Gold that is on Them, Nor Taketh Unto Thee, Lest Thou be a Snare Theirin: For it is Abomination to the LORD Thy GOD.

By the way, in Hebrew, the word abomination means disgusting, another translation to throw-up. Wow!!! Verse 26 reads,

Neither Shalt Thou Bring an Abomination into Thy House, Lest Thou be a Cursed Thing Like It. But Thou Shalt Utterly Detest it and Thou Shalt Utterly Abhor it for it is a Cursed Thing.

It is crystal clear isn't it? I remember when I was growing up that the famous Elvis Presley was raised up by his mother and father in a Baptist Church. He was a fine young man. In the prime of his life, in the fast lane, Hollywood and fame put a hook in him. Tommy Barnett is a pastor of a very large church in Arizona. He has over 20,000 strong and his son Mathew Barnett has the LARGEST RESCUE MISSION IN THE WORLD, located in Los Angeles. He told me a story that when Elvis Presley was in his twenties, Pastor Tommy Barnett pleaded with Elvis and told him, "Elvis, come serve the Lord and sing for him."

From Mafia Boss to the Cross

Elvis Presley responded, "No, I am the King of Rock and Roll." And it is true, he became a king, and he became an IDOL for millions and millions of teenagers in America. Then his fame was struck down at 43 with alcohol and drugs and a needle in his arm. His life ended and we do not know whether he went up or down. What about you? Whose idol do you want to be? There are two kinds of armies in the world: Satan's army and God's army. Which one do you want to be? Joshua said, "Me and my house we serve the Lord" What about you?

Now it was about 11:30 at night and in Simon's apartment, believe it or not, he had idols. He had some that were 50 pounds and some that weighed 100 pounds. Some that were metal and some that were dipped in gold. Simon was about to be free. He was making his stand for God. What a brave young man. The process began. Linda, Rose and Lydia were praying intercession prayer. The Bible declares that behind every idol there is a dedicated demon sent from hell. We began to smash the idols and put them into potato sacks. We would drag them outside to the dumpster. There were four statues of Buddah's image. They were marble and they could not easily be broken. That's when I got the idea of dumping them over the Brooklyn bridge. This one 60 pound idol, we agreed, to put in the car and dump over the bridge. We were rejoicing. Simon asked to be water baptized. He kindly asked us if we would water baptize him in his home. We dunked him in the water and he came out fresh like a dove. Then I remember five of us driving to the Brooklyn bridge and dumping Buddha and the idols over the bridge. I thank God that he protected us. Why? Because if the police would have saw us they would have wondered if we were dumping a body over. We really would have had problems explaining it. Can you imagine what it would look like if the police stopped us? How could they possibly believe what we were up to? They would say that we were out of our minds and maybe we would make the seven o'clock news. There have been other incidents where our ministry has had the privilege and honor to meet and expand in New York City. Simon's situation was a blessing!

ORDINATION OF POLICE LIEUTENANT, N.Y.C.

Richard Rinaldo and his wife Mariana, I am happy to say, have been very good friends and supporters of the work that God has entrusted to me. Richard, about fifteen years ago on a mission trip to Romania, fell in love with a beautiful young lady that loves the Lord and people. Immediately after the wedding in Romania they reunited and resided in New York City. She owns a very exclusive beauty shop and she stands in the faith of Christ. With her work and her personality she illuminates people's lives everywhere she goes. Richard is a Lieutenant in the New York City district and a mighty man of God. Richard is also a body guard for Morris Cerullo Ministries. He was born in New York City and he serves the community faithfully, keeping the law, and defending the faith. We had the privilege in 2005 to ordain them both into the ministry. As you read the stories in this book you know that, at one time, I was being bribed by the police and even Lieutenants and Sergeants. But now I am going a different direction by ordaining police into Christ's army so they too can enforce the law with power from above. To clean up the city and to rescue victims with the love of God and not with violence and physical abuse. There is no room for that anymore!! Everlasting Chip Ministry wishes to give a warm and sincere thanks to Richard Rinaldo and family. We believe that they have an impact on the people of the 'Big Apple.'

CLOSE CALL: UNITED STATES IMMIGRATION

I want to express my gratitude and thanks from the bottom of my heart to the Lord Jesus Christ for working a miracle of his mercy in my life. This brief story I want to share with you reader, hoping that it will impact your life if you are going through a similar situation. I want to begin by declaring that all my family are American citizens except me. Even now, I hold a green card, for permanent residence. It is only by the mercy of God and the wonderful laws of America that I am granted permanent residence. You see, America has the constitution, which is based on Christianity and the Bible. The other nations do not have that. We are blessed with good laws, the best laws! Anyone that comes from another country must have a history of good conduct for a minimum of five years. Then they can apply for a naturalization document. However, in my life as a young man there were many tragedies. The pages of my life have turned against me. I have not become a naturalized citizen. As the years went by I tried to become a citizen. I applied in 1993 and I was rejected due to my criminal record. The funny thing is that I was never convicted of a felony. The majority of my convictions were misdemeanors. Because of my guilt I procrastinated but I never gave up praying. I kept hoping that God would make a miracle

He did. His ways are not our ways. I was told to wait until 2001. During these years I had the privilege of bringing the Gospel to more than 18 nations. This work was sponsored by the good people in America. As you know, I have conducted many seminars. I have ministered to Governors, Presidents, Mayors and Senators, movie stars, lawyers and doctors. I have ministered to rich people and poor people and the homeless. Thirty-seven times God has sent me into China to make a declaration to them that: America loves you! America is not a place, it is a choice. We don't live in America, America lives in our hearts. America is a nation built on 'GOD WE TRUST." I have done my duty. It has been more than 21 years. I can happily say I haven't even had a parking ticket. I have fed the homeless. I have trained and discipled people and ordained more than 800 people under the banner of the United States. I have visited the hospitals and have gone to the jails to minister. Oh, what a pleasure to bring the good news to them.

Yet, there is one thing in my heart that I must overcome. That is to become an American Citizen. I knew that sooner or later I had to face Immigration. Even though I am redeemed and forgiven by God, now I must prove it to the law of the land. I was hoping that my morality, my character would both justify and satisfy the leaders of the United States. I continued to travel under the status of my green card but my time of confrontation was close at hand. After 911, when the enemy struck in New York City and we all suffered greatly, I was more determined to preach the Gospel to the Islamic people. Why? Because they want to send bombs but we must continue, as missionaries, to go to the front line territories to bring the Gospel. And to bring the good news that America was founded by GOD. The gospel and democracy brings liberty to ALL. Not just to some. I had just returned from 30 days in Malaysia where I preached to thousands of people, telling them of the Good News of the Lord Jesus Christ, and that AMERICA LOVES THEM!!! I am pleased to say that the Prime Minister of Malaysia and his wife, and the ambassador of Malaysia, welcomed me with open arms and allowed me to be the guest speaker in the Royal Palace.

On my re-entry into the United States I realized that president Bush declared to Customs to check and screen anyone that had a past record.

Dr. Bruno Caporrimo

As we landed at Los Angeles International Airport I was wearing a Chinese coat. When the deputy checked my green card, he stamped my passport, and he greeted me to come in as usual. But then he hesitated. He looked at me and he looked at my Chinese wife. He responded by asking me a question. He asked me, "You were born in Italy, married a Chinese wife and you've been in Malaysia." I could read his mind. He thought that I was a radical Islamic. He asked, "Where have you been the last three months?" My response was, "Hong Kong, Taiwan, China, Malaysia and Singapore." He took my green card back and pointed to the floor and said, "Follow the yellow line." They released my wife and they kept me for 6 hours.

They put me in this little temporary jail. There were over 50 people there from many different nations; Germany, Korea, Italy, China, and Japan. The Chief-of-Police gave me a brief interrogation. He was a Filipino man who spoke broken English. With a very firm voice he said, "What do you do for a living?" I said, "I am a Pastor and an Evangelist." He replied firmly, "Like hell you are!" He used God's name in vain. He added, "You're nothing but a gangster. We have your record here." I said, "No, that was more than 40 years ago. I have been redeemed." He did not believe it and threw me in a cell with all these people. I felt like the ceiling fell on top of my head. My dark hour was coming. Judgment was coming to me. I was about to reap some of the evils that I had done in my prior life. The Bible declares in Colossians 6:7 that whatever you sow you shall reap. Now it is my turn. I found out that Immigration is the highest law in the country!! Even though my crimes were 40 years ago and I was redeemed by society and I was reinstated by the laws of the land and the court system, I must still prove my integrity. I must give a full explanation to Immigration.

I found myself in this room waiting my turn. There were more than 50 people waiting ahead of me. I was being questioned as a result of a United Nations mandate and the cooperation of President Bush. The deputies were only doing there job. They looked at the record and they thought, "I was a big fish." I sat in the cell and I opened up the Bible. I began to send quick e-mails to heaven. I remember that Jesus said in the Bible, "They will kick you out of Synagogues and they will put you in jails for my name's sake. But do not be afraid what to say, your Heavenly Father will put words in your mouth." Once again I was desperate and frustrated. A downtime came into my life again. While in my deep devotion in that cell, I kneeled down, I took a blanket and put it over my head. I heard the gentle voice of the Holy Spirit saying to me, "Read Proverbs 29:26." It says, "Many seek the rulers favor: but every man's judgment comes from the Lord." This is the King James translation. I was reading from my personal Bible called, 'The Word", which has 26 translations. Another translation from NEB reads, "Many seek audience of a prince, but in every case the Lord decides it."

Wow, this passage quickly took away all my fears. The Chief-of-police did not know my case. I looked at him. There he was drinking beer on the job. He mocked me, judged me and used God's name in vain. You see, I needed to look to the Master. I kneeled down and I said a quick prayer. I said, "Thank you dear Lord. You put me inside here and you will defend me and you will get me out. I belong to you Lord. You rule and reign in America. Amen." I remember I took the blanket off my head. It was 1:00 in the morning and it was raining outside. My sweet bride was somewhere in the airport suffering and waiting for me. Lydia was raised in a fine family. She is more righteous than I am. She graduated from Christ College in Taiwan. She holds a Masters Degree in Speech and Administration. She worked with China News for many years and faithfully served the communities. She married me and gave everything up to live by faith, by becoming a Missionary.

It is about 1 a.m. and Immigration is busy checking everyone in to U.S. soil. They were busy at work to protect our borders. There was a young man there who was about 25 years old. He said, "I am a Mormon." Another one said to me, "I am a Jehovah's Witness." We began to discuss theology and I became very fortunate. They asked me to pray for them. I did and I pointed them both to Christ. Suddenly my sorrow became joy. I began to say, "Thank you Lord for putting me inside this cell. You used Joseph in the Bible and you can use me now." My time came and one of the Filipino deputies opened the cell and led me into a private room. He sat me next to his desk and he began to type. He said, "I believe you are a Pastor, however, I must do my job. You have a long criminal record and I must write down a report." He added, "Go all the way back, 45 years ago, when you first came from Italy." My response was, "It has been so long ago that I do not remember anything." I responded to him the best way that I could concerning my past. Then I began to boast about the works of God and all his miracles in my life. He replied to me, "Wow, you are more righteous than I am. I am just a Filipino. I am an immigrant just like you and I work for the Government."

I said to him, "No, only Jesus Christ is righteous and you can be righteous in Him. Romans 10: 9-10 says, 'That if you confess with your mouth that God raised Jesus from the dead, and believe in your heart you shall be saved. For with your mouth confession is made and with your heart you turn unto righteousness.' There's nothing good about us. I am a sinner just like you, saved by grace." I watched him and, to my surprise, he got up and adjusted his belt and walked towards the door. He shut the door and walked up to me and said, "Please Pastor Bruno, I want you to pray for me. I want to accept Jesus Christ." Wow, every single time that Satan messed me up, God would always raise me up!

He made me sign some documents. He kept my green card and he replied to me that I was being released on parole. I said, "What do you mean parole?" He said, "I am doing my duty. You have been released on parole until you go in front of an Immigration judge." One month later I received a letter that I was scheduled for deportation. My God, they wanted to deport me. My church and all my students began to pray. Day after day and night after night we prayed. One of my dearest friends, Ben Lofstedt, is an attorney and a very good one. He and his wife Sally have been my friends for more than 20 years. He called me and he told me that God told him that he was going to defend me. The time came and at 9 a.m. we entered the room of the Immigration judge. I remember the very words that the judge declared. He said, "I am an Immigration judge. I have the power to judge your case and to deport you or keep you here." Over a year had passed because of technicalities. There were many documents involved and much red tape. During this time many people, Pastors and leaders in the community, wrote many wonderful letters vouching for my character and contributions to the community and society. These included California State Christian University, Pomona Bible College and Crystal Cathedral. As well as some local people in my community. On the day of the trial the District Attorney had an F.B.I. record. All the records were submitted, including this F.B.I. report. The judge evaluated the case and asked me, "What would you do if we deport you to Italy?" I replied, "Your honor, District

Attorney and people of the United States, my life is in your hands. Your honor the God of Abraham, Isaac and Jacob, who ordained you to be a judge of the United States Immigration, has called me to preach the Gospel all over the world. If you deport me to Italy I will go there and preach the Gospel to the Italians. However, your honor, I believe that God has called me to preach the Gospel here in America as well. America lives in my heart. It is the best country in the world. We have the best laws in the world, GOD'S LAWS. I owe the American people my life. I want to serve them with every fiber in my body. I want to help the new generations to think right and to do right. To serve America with integrity and honesty which come purely from God."

The judge looked at me, he looked at the District Attorney and responded, "I will wipe everything out and restore you and give you status FOREVER as a law abiding citizen. All your past is wiped out and I order you to get your green card back and proceed to become a naturalized citizen." He added, "You are from Italy. You had good conduct but it was the people and the crime in New York City that caused you to go astray. We are responsible for rehabilitating you into a law abiding citizen." He added, "However you will never come before me for the same charges. If you become corrupt again, then next time, it will not be so easy." I had a joy in my heart and tears in my eyes. The God of heaven sent his Angel and the Holy Spirit through this wonderful judge and District Attorney. I was reinstated with a new lease on life. Remember that when you face a mountain and you cannot climb over, go around or go underneath, until you get through. Only with GOD WILL YOU FULFILL YOUR DREAM IN YOUR LIFE!!

25
2005, AUGUST 17: ANOTHER BLOWOUT!

Six days prior to my 30th mission to China, the schedule was set and the itinerary ready. Then on August 17th, 3:30 p.m., Peter Whitney one of the students in my class, received a citation of blocking traffic from the airport police because at his arrival to the airport he had a flat tire. When we asked the police officer to help him, instead he received this undeserving citation. He asked me if I would be a witness to him. I replied, 'Yes". On August 17th, at 4:30 he was scheduled to be in court. I remember that afternoon, at 3 p.m., we left the University parking lot heading to Irvine. He was driving on Jamboree blvd., which is a five lane highway. He was driving on the right hand lane. I was sitting on the back seat and I was trying to take a nap. I never dreamed or even thought about what was about to take place in my life. Peter said to me, "Dr. Bruno, I think we passed the court house." I looked up and saw to my left that there was a gas station at the corner of the intersection. I said, "No problem, we'll go to the gas station and ask the people where the court house is."

At this point I would like to say something about Peter Whitney. He was introduced to the school and to me by my good friend. His desire was to be trained and to be licensed to become a pastor. His character was very polite. He was a well spoken individual and a gentlemen. He did not drink, he did not smoke and he loved people. He truly has a heart to serve others. My heart went out to him. I could have written a note to the judge, but I decided to go there personally. Now, in this moment while were driving, I expected him to look in the mirror, signal, wait for clearance and merge to the left lane. Instead he did something that was not normal. I would call it cowboy driving. He turned the wheel to the left at 90 degrees, accelerated through all four lanes and accelerated to 70 m.p.h. at the same time. He turned the wheel so fast that you could here his wrists pounding on the wheel. Jokingly I said, "Oh, New York Taxi driver!"

Within two seconds the driver behind us, hit us at 60 m.p.h. The van flipped three times over the dividing lane. The impact of the first flip was so powerful that I heard the bang of metal to metal and contact with the pavement. It sounded like an explosion. I flew out of the drivers side window even though I had my seatbelt on. The impact was so powerful that, with the law of gravity, I flew like a bird. Even the seatbelt didn't keep me. I landed over the divider on the other side of the highway. I broke three ribs, my kneecaps, and my elbows. When I landed to the ground the only thing I remember saying was, "Lord, but what about the ministry. I am going to die." When I landed I said, "Wow, thank you Lord. I'm okay" Well, lo and behold, the van rolled three times and fell on top of me. It squashed my ribs and one of the ribs put a hole in my lungs. Before I passed out I said, "Jesus, help me!!" Within seconds there were police and ambulance all over the place. I was in trauma. The pain was indescribable. I came to and Jesse, the front passenger, was weeping over me. I was losing my life and I was going down fast. Paramedics put oxygen in my mouth immediately. I remember the car rolling on me and an Angel of the Lord moving the car away from me. You see, in Psalms 91:11, it declares that; God gives his angels charge over us.

The enemy caused this accident by confusing the driver in his misbehavior. But God intervened for my life. I came to and was surrounded by many Doctors in the emergency room. One of the Doctors said, "Pastor Bruno we have to operate on you right away. You have a three inch hole in one of your lungs. We have to operate on you and put a tube in it, so the air can go in your lungs." My response was, "No, call my wife and have them pray for me." The Doctor responded, "By ten in the morning you will be dead." I said, "Doctor, please give me until 9 in the morning, then you can do your surgery." More than 50 people around the nation, I found out, were praying for me. At Nine o'clock in the morning they put me into a scanner machine and the doctor came out with the x-ray. He said, "You received a miracle, the hole in your lungs is gone." Glory to God. I know that my God is real. Only believe. If you believe, there is a miracle around the corner waiting for you. I admit this accident shook me. The doctor said that the ribs would heal in six months naturally, by a slow process. Today is March, 2007. I can declare that my ribs are 90% restored.

This is my testimony; FROM MAFIA BOSS TO THE CROSS. I'm going to continue to defend the faith. Jesus Christ is Lord of all! I believe the best is yet to come. God has a plan for your life. Please come on board and follow His dream for your life!

NOTE FROM THE AUTHOR

From the age of five to twelve I lived with a neighbor, a friend of the family by the name of Giovanni La Rosa. This family owned a castle that sits on five acres on the outskirts of Palermo. They raised me up and educated me and they mentored me. He was my Godfather as a child. In the year 2000, after 40 years, they contacted me and told me the good news. I had inherited the castle. In 2001 I visited my Godfather, Giovanni La Rosa. He was very, very, sick with a liver problem. He informed me that I needed 800,000.00 to pay taxes that were due on the property. The land and the castle are valued at 60 million dollars. He encouraged me to take over quickly. He said the time was very short. If I did not come up with the money, that the city would sell it. The mafia, they have defiled some of the government leaders. They would take over. Tragedy occurred again. I neglected, I procrastinated. I was hoping that I would get the money. I thought, "Sooner or later, I will get it" Instead, in 2005, I called the La Rosa family and his wife told me that my Godfather passed away. She said that the doctor that was taking care of him gave an offer of half a million dollars and took over the castle. I admit and repent that I was not too wise. I could have gone to many lenders and negotiated them into partnership to pay the debt off. Instead, I didn't do anything. I only hoped that I would get the money. The money did not come. The doctor is fixing and remodeling the castle. Who knows, maybe this book, 'Mafia Boss to the Cross' will be a movie! Then I can get the money and redeem the castle back. But why? Because I am not giving up. I am not looking back. Even though I lost it all, I am willing to give it all again and again, to serve the Lord.

The kingdom of God is like a pearl, you give up everything, to get it. When you give Him all, then He gives you all that He has. This is a father and son relationship. So, I am going forward. I believe the best is yet to come because the testing is over and the blessings are coming down with signs and wonders. Mentally, physically and financially we will be blessed and even the castle could be redeemed back!!

I would like to turn the castle into a Training Center and Bible College. To train and equip the Italian people and to build an army for the Lord Jesus Christ. By the way, if you have the money and you want a partnership in this adventure please contact me.

'CONFESSION OF FAITH'

I am now releasing my faith, by confessing this to be the greatest day of my life. "This is the day that the Lord hath made, I will rejoice and be glad in it." I am a re-created being. Old things have passed away and all things have become new. I am created into his glorious image and likeness. I am his workmanship and am complete in Christ.

I am full of his Spirit and divine power. I am God's property. I have been bought with the blood of the Lord Jesus Christ; therefore, I am free from the corpse of the law. Sin, sickness, poverty, fear, doubt, worry, confusion and everything Satan represents shall not have dominion over me. I am prospering in my spirit, soul, body and finances, for I am a liberated person. Jesus said that I will know the truth and that the truth will make me free.

I am standing fast in the liberty wherein Christ has made me free. I am expecting God to meet all of my needs and to do super abundantly above all I dare to ask, hope, dream or desire in every area of my life. I speak directly to every mountain of satanic adversity in my life and command them to go in the name of Jesus, they cannot stay, and they must go, in Jesus' name. Through the abundance of God's grace, I have received the gift of righteousness, for I am the righteousness of God in Christ and am now reigning in life by Christ Jesus. Today I will worship with all my heart, soul, and strength. I lift up my voice and hands in praise and adoration to his glorious name, for He is worthy of praise and He has made me worthy to praise His name.

(CONFESSION OF FAITH- Excerpt from "Strength for the Journey" written by Dr. Henry B. Alexander, Senior pastor, Shield of Faith Ministry, Pomona, Ca.)

Everlasting Chip Ministry University International

Mission FIRE Statement: To win 200,000,000 souls

1. Carry the saving and healing message of Jesus Christ to every nation and island on the earth.
2. Proclaim the whole gospel of Jesus Christ to every person on the earth in our generation.
3. Build-up, train, and strengthen believers in every nation by birthing the prophet in them.
4. Conduct school's of Ministry and open campuses for the purpose of passing the a anointing God gave to Bruno Caporrimo, to us. So we can reach their villages, communities, cities and nations for Christ.
5. Present the witness that Jesus is the Messiah to every creature; black, white or yellow.
6. Maximize technology, people and resources which God has provided for the spreading of the gospel.
7. Build God's mighty, active army of trained believers in every nation for the purpose of overtaking darkness and spreading the light of the gospel of Jesus Christ.

8. Establish a prayer covering over the entire earth with strategically located prayer centers which continually offer up prayer for the nations.
9. Provide prayer command centers in homes so that individuals and the hurting masses of the world will know that we are his disciples.
10. Recognize and support the unity in the body of Christ so the world will know that we are His disciples.
11. Operate, articulate and demonstrate to the world the 5-fold ministries of the church as outlined in Ephesians 4:11, for the perfecting of the saints, for the work of the ministry and edifying of the body of Christ.
12. To bring honor and glory to God in everything we do and say. In every action of the ministry.

I Corinthians 15:58

BRIEF BIOGRAPHY

Dr. Bruno was born in Palermo, Sicily. He is the second youngest of a family of seven. During World War II his family lost everything and they were exiled to the United States when he was fifteen years old. Within two years tragedy struck again and both of his parents died. Dr. Caporrimo slipped into a depression during which time he lost his identity and the values of life that he had learned from his family. He was then caught up in the world's fast lane for twenty years. During this time he became involved with the Italian mafia and became a habitual lawbreaker, breaking the laws of both country and God.

At the age of 43, after experiencing more unhappiness and tragedy, he cried out to the Lord. God heard his cries and opened the door to eternal life. He gave Dr. Bruno a spiritual anointing, baptized him with the Holy Spirit, and transformed him with his love. Dr. Bruno was caught up in the heavens and was inspired and commissioned by God to build a spiritual army. More than twenty years have gone by and God has done incredible things in the life of Dr. Bruno Caporrimo. During the twenty years he has earned a Doctor of Divinity degree from Living Word Bible College located in Pomona, California. He has obtained a Certificate from Billy Graham's School of Evanglism as well as another Doctorate degree in Theology from California State Christian University. He has founded a school of Biblical Theology which is in affiliation with California State Christian University. Additionally, Dr. Caporrimo is a Board Certified Psychotherapist and Counsellor by the Evangelical Order of Pastoral Counsellors of America.

He and his wife, Lydia Caporrimo, have traveled throughout more than 18 nations as Missionaries. He has written more than ten inspirational books and developed a curriculum for his Bible College. He has conducted numerous conferences, seminars and healing crusades. He has conducted 37 Mission trips to China. God has blessed Dr. Bruno Caporrimo with a Prophetic Ministry to deliver God's Word and the saving knowledge of Jesus Christ to millions of people. His own unique spiritual journey has touched the lives of many thousands of people through supernatural healings and life-changing prophecies.

LIST OF BOOKS AVAILABLE

Honeymoon with the Holy Spirit
available in English & Chinese

The Gift of Prophecy
available in English & Chinese

The Snake in the Glass
available in English, Chinese & Italian

Hermeneutics
available in Chinese

God's Plan for Man
available in English & Chinese

Birthing the Prophet in You

The Invisible War
available in English, Chinese & Italian

Understanding Your Spiritual Gifts

Deliverance & Healing for All

**Please go to our website to place orders or to support the orphanages:
http: //www.drbrunoecm.net**

Call us for speaking engagements or crusades:
(714) 772-7802

Everlasting CHIP Ministry Discipleship & Training Center invites you to our Corespondence School of Theology to license you for Ministry. We are a accredited training center committed to equipping the SAINTS! For more information please contact us. God bless you !

Printed in the United States
90560LV00004B/29/A